HISTORY

of the

Early Settlement and Progress

of

Cumberland County

NEW JERSEY

and of the

CURRENCY

of

THIS *and the* ADJOINING COLONIES

Lucius Q. C. Elmer

HERITAGE BOOKS
2011

HERITAGE BOOKS

AN IMPRINT OF HERITAGE BOOKS, INC.

Books, CDs, and more—Worldwide

For our listing of thousands of titles see our website
at
www.HeritageBooks.com

A Facsimile Reprint
Published 2011 by
HERITAGE BOOKS, INC.
Publishing Division
100 Railroad Ave. #104
Westminster, Maryland 21157

Entered according to the Act of Congress in the year
one thousand eight hundred and sixty-nine, by
George F. Nixon
In the Clerk's Office of the District Court of the District of New Jersey

International Standard Book Numbers
Paperbound: 978-1-55613-019-9
Clothbound: 978-0-7884-8629-6

"In *A Rwandan Bishop's Confession*, Joel Kubwimana demonstrates quite persuasively how essential the mother tongue is in the reconceptualization of society. By doing this monumental work, he has succeeded in placing the name of Aloys Bigirumwami on the list of notable scholars on the African continent who continue to advocate for the use of African languages in scholarly discourse. A good read!"

—**Philip Tetteh Laryea**, Associate Professor of African Theology,
Akrofi-Christaller Institute, Ghana

"This is a great book, worthy to be read. Kubwimana clearly explores the life and works of Bishop Aloys Bigirumwami and points out the vital role of vernacular language and traditional beliefs in contextualizing Christian faith in contemporary Africa, particularly in Rwanda. I highly recommend this book to all theologians, clergy, lay leaders, and church planters pursuing Christian faith for the contemporary generation to be able to understand and accept the gospel, thus becoming Jesus's disciples and taking on the call to spread the Christian faith to the next generation."

—**Niyonzima Samvura Jean Damascene**, President and Legal
Representative, Harvest Bible Fellowship, Rwanda

PREFACE.

THESE sketches of the early history of Cumberland County were prepared a few years ago for the columns of a newspaper. Many of the facts detailed, relating to the first settlers and proprietors, came to the knowledge of the writer in the course of a somewhat protracted career as a lawyer. Although of no great importance, it has been thought they were worth preserving in a more permanent and accessible form. Having been born in Bridgeton, when it contained only three hundred inhabitants, and always resided there, he has witnessed, and had the opportunity of minutely stating, its growth into a city of no mean importance.

The chapter giving a history of the money of account and of circulation, in this and the adjoining colonies, from their beginnings to a recent date, it is believed embraces facts not to be found in any of our histories, which were fast passing into oblivion, but which are too curious and instructive to be entirely lost.

BRIDGETON, May, 1869.

EARLY HISTORY

OF

CUMBERLAND COUNTY, NEW JERSEY.

CHAPTER I.

EARLY SETTLERS AND PROPRIETORS.

CUMBERLAND COUNTY was set off from the county of Salem, and erected into a new county, by an act of assembly passed January 19, 1747–8. The Duke of Cumberland, who had not long before gained the victory of Culloden, and thereby established the house of Hanover permanently on the throne of Great Britain, was the great hero of the day, and the new county was named after him.

The first settlers of this part of West Jersey were probably Dutch and Swedes. Gabriel Thomas, a Friend, who lived for a few years in Pennsylvania, on his return to England in 1698, published an account of that province and of West New Jersey. Describing the rivers, he names Prince Maurice River, "where the Swedes used to kill the geese in great numbers for their feathers only, leaving their carcasses behind them." Quite a number of Swedes settled in the neighborhood of this river, and engaged in hunting and cutting lumber, without, however, obtaining a title to the soil, until some of them purchased of the English. About the year 1743, a Swedish church was built on the east side of Maurice River, nearly opposite Buckshootem, where missionaries were accustomed to preach until after the Revolution. The graveyard with a few stones still remains. Many of the Swedish names have been continued in the neighborhood.

A few of the New Haven people, who as early as 1641 made a settlement on the creek called by the Dutch Varcken's Kill (now Salem Creek), may have wandered into the limits of Cumberland,

2

and thus become the pioneers of the considerable number, who about fifty years later came from Connecticut, Rhode Island, and Long Island.

The Indians do not appear to have been numerous, consisting mostly of wandering tribes, having no permanent settlements, and no principal sachem or chief. There was a considerable tribe which generally resided in Stow Creek and Greenwich, where many of their stone hatchets and other relics have been found. At the place still called Indian Fields, about a mile northeast of Bridgeton, they had a settlement before 1697, the place being referred to by that name in a survey of that date. Another contemporaneous survey referred to a settlement on the Cohansey, in Upper Hopewell, about a quarter of a mile below the mill known as Seeley's Mill. There was also a settlement on the west side of the same river, just above Bridgeton, on the property now belonging to the iron and nail works; and the tradition is that an Indian chief was buried, or, as some accounts say, placed in a box or coffin, on the limbs of a tree, on the point of land opposite North Street, since from that tradition called "Coffin Point." Other places of settlement or occasional places of resort are known to have existed near Fairton, and on Maurice River.

Fenwick purchased the land of these, and to the fair and reasonble treatment they received from the Friends, who were the first English settlers, may probably be ascribed the absence of those desolating wars which prevailed in New England. But this circumstance has prevented much notice being taken of the aborigines in the early accounts of West Jersey. James Daniels, a minister among the Friends, whose father settled in the forks of Stow Creek, near the place now called Canton, in Salem County, in 1690, when he was about five years old, learned the Indian language, and says in his memoirs, "the white people were few, and the natives a multitude; they were a sober, grave, and temperate people, and used no manner of oath in their speech; but as the country grew older the people grew worse, and had corrupted the natives in their morals, teaching them bad words, and the excessive use of strong drink." Thomas, in his account of West Jersey before referred to, says "the Dutch and Swedes inform us that they greatly decreased in numbers to what they were when they came into this country, and the Indians themselves say that two of them die to every one Christian that comes in here." The minutes of the justices and freeholders of Cumberland County for the year 1754, state that a charge of £4, 3s. 4d. was brought by Deerfield Township, for taking care of an old Indian who died in said precinct, which was allowed. At a conference held by commissioners appointed by the legislature with the Indians in 1758, one Robert Kecot claimed " the township of Deerfield, in the county of Cumberland, where the Presbyterian meeting-house stands, and also the tracts of James Wasse, Joseph Peck, and Stephen Chesup." After this, all the Indian claims were fully paid for and relinquished. A few of the descendants of these original inhabitants lingered within the county until after the Revolution, earning their subsistence principally by making baskets. Soon after the commencement of the present century they had all removed or died.

All vacant lands being—according to the law of Great Britain— vested in the crown, and it being the established principle of European law that countries uninhabited, or inhabited only by savages, became the property of the nation taking possession, King Charles II. granted all that territory, called by the Dutch New Netherlands, including part of the State of New York, and all New Jersey, to his brother, the Duke of York, afterwards James II., March 12, 1663-4. The duke conveyed New Jersey to Lord Berkeley and Sir George Carteret, June 24, 1664. In 1672, the Dutch reconquered the province; but in 1673 it was restored, and new grants were executed. Berkley, in 1673, conveyed his half to John Fenwick, and shortly afterwards Fenwick conveyed nine-tenth parts of his half to William Penn, Gawen Lawrie, and Nicholas Lucas, in trust for the creditors of Edward Billing. The above-named persons had all become followers of George Fox, and were then called Quakers, adopting themselves the name of Friends. Fenwick had been a member of a church of Independents, whereof John Goodwin was the pastor. He held a commission as major of cavalry, which Johnson, in his *History of Salem*, says was written in Cromwell's own hand.

In 1676, the province was divided, Fenwick, Penn, Lawrie, and Lucas becoming proprietors of the half called West Jersey. Billing—who was a London merchant—having failed, his nine-tenths, held by Penn and others, was conveyed to his creditors and others in hundredth parts, or, as the deeds made in England set it forth, in nineteenth parts of ninety hundredth parts, so that a full proprietary interest came to be reckoned a hundredth part. Lesser parts of the hundredths, or a definite number of acres therein, were also frequently conveyed to individuals. Fenwick, and Eldridge, and Warner, to whom he executed a long lease in England, for the purpose of raising money, were recognized as owning ten proprietaries, or one-tenth of the province. It would seem that each particular hundredth was at first in some way designated, and the respective owners drew lots for their several shares; but this designation was never fully carried out, and it is not known how the parts were owned. Fenwick's ten proprietaries, however, were all considered to be contained in what was called the Salem tenth, extending from Berkeley River (now Oldman's Creek) to a creek a little east of the Cohansey, originally called the Tweed, which, having a wide mouth where it empties into the Delaware, was supposed to be a stream commencing far up to the north, but which proved to be confined to the marsh, and has since been called Back Creek.

Fenwick came into the Delaware in June, 1675, with his family and servants, consisting of two daughters and their husbands, one unmarried daughter, and two servants. His wife remained in England, and never came to America. Edward Champney, one of his sons-in-law, brought with him three servants, one of whom was Mark Reeve, who settled at Greenwich, and built a house not far from the Cohansey, near the house where John Sheppard long lived. The servants, as is remarked by Smith, in his *History of New Jersey*, being accustomed to work, and willing to encounter the hardships and privations incident to the settlement of a new country, succeeded much better than their masters. Mark Reeve, among others, became a considerable proprietor, and is still represented by numerous respectable descendants.

So far as is now known, the Dutch and Swedes never took any steps to secure a permanent title to the land upon which they settled, and did not even take deeds from the Indians. Whatever title they may have claimed as the first settlers and improvers, was ignored by the English, although there is reason to believe they were, in many cases, permitted to become purchasers at the usual price for the unimproved land. A few names apparently not English are found among the early freeholders.

Penn and the other legal proprietors of West Jersey, in 1676, signed an agreement the original of which, well engrossed on vellum, in a bound quarto volume, is preserved in the land office at Burlington, regulating the government and the mode of disposing of the lands. It provided for dividing the territory into tenths, originally intended to take the place of counties, and the tenths were to be divided into hundredths. Fenwick did not sign this agreement, but assumed to act independently of the other proprietors, which was the occasion of much contention. Salem, however, was always recognized as one of the tenths, and Fenwick, or his grantees, as the owners of ten proprietaries. During part of his life he claimed to be sole or chief proprietor of the moiety of New Jersey, and established his government at the place he called New Salem, now the city of Salem. He appointed a Secretary and Surveyor General, the latter being at first Richard Hancock, who came over with him. In 1678 James Nevill was appointed Secretary, and his son-in-law, Samuel Hedge, Surveyor General, Hancock having favored the claims of the other proprietors, and acted under them.

In 1682 Fenwick conveyed all his interest in New Jersey to William Penn, except the part which was called Fenwick's colony, containing, as was supposed, 150,000 acres. When he died in the latter part of 1683, he appointed Penn and others his executors, giving them "full power to lett, sett, sell and dispose" of his whole estate, for the paying of his debts and improving his estate, for his heirs during their non age. By virtue of the aforesaid deed and will, Penn and the other executors made conveyances of large parcels of land, besides what Fenwick had himself conveyed, by virtue of which surveys were made, and under which the titles are held.

There seems to have been for several years after Fenwick's arrival, a constant conflict between him and the Assembly, which at length occasioned his deed to Penn in 1682. In May, 1683, he appeared himself as a member of the Assembly, and it was then enacted as a law that the lands and marsh or meadow formerly laid out for Salem Town bounds, by agreement of John Fenwick and the people of Salem Liberty, shall stand and be forever to and for the only use of the freeholders and inhabitants of said town. It was then agreed *nem. con.*, "only John Fenwick excepted his tenth, which he said then at that time was not under the same circumstances, but now freely consenteth thereunto," that the concessions agreed on in 1676, should be the fundamentals and ground of the government of West Jersey.

This assent, however, does not seem to have been understood by Fenwick as hindering him from disposing of his land, without regard to the agreements or concessions or laws. His will, an ancient copy of which is before me, dated August 7, 1683, made on his sick bed at Fenwick's Grove, professes to dispose of large manors and tracts of land to his grand-children. It contains this clause: "Item: I give and bequeath to my three grand-children and their heirs male forever, all that tract of land laying near the river heretofore called Cohansey, which I will have hereafter called Cæsaria River, and which is known by the name of the Town Neck; and my will is that it, together with the land on the other side which is called Shrewsbury Neck, and other the lands thereunto belonging, which is contained in my Indian purchase, and so up the bay to the mouth of Monmouth River (Alloway's Creek was then so called), and up Monmouth River to the head or farthest branch thereof, and so in a straight line to the head of Cæsaria River, all which I will to be called the manor of Cæsaria, and that there shall be a city erected, and marshes and land allowed as my executors shall see convenient, which I empower them to do and to name the land; further, my will is that out of the residue of the land and marshes shall be divided equally among my said heirs, and that Fenwick's dividend shall join to the town and Bacon's Creek, where, my will is, there shall be a house erected and called the Manor house, for keeping of courts." This manor, it will be seen, embraced the present townships of Greenwich, Hopewell, Cohansey and Stow Creek in Cumberland, Lower Alloway's Creek, and part of Upper Alloway's Creek Townships in Salem; but, like many other magnificent projects, it was never carried out. None of his grants or devises of specific parcels of land, except Salem Town, have been recognized as valid; and no titles under them are good, unless regular surveys have been made and recorded, or such a length of actual possession has been had as to bar a rival claimant.

Directly after Fenwick's arrival, he provided for laying out a neck of land for a town at Cohansey, one-half for the chief proprietor (himself), and one-half for the purchasers, the lots to be sixteen acres each. The town thus projected was called by the settlers Greenwich, although it continued for many years to be also called Cohansey. A memorial of the proprietors of East and West Jersey to the crown, dated in 1701, prays that the port of Perth Amboy, in East

Jersey, and the ports of Burlington and Cohansey, in West Jersey, may be established ports of those respective provinces forever. An act of the Assembly of West Jersey, in 1695, recites that a considerable number of people are settled on or about Cohansey, *alias* Cæsaria River, within the county of Salem, and enacts that there shall be two fairs kept yearly at the town of Greenwich at Cohansey aforesaid; the first on the 24th and 25th days of April, and the second on the 16th and 17th days of October. These fairs were continued and were largely attended until 1765, when a law was enacted reciting that fairs in the town of Greenwich had been found inconvenient and unnecessary, and that therefore no fairs should be hereafter held there. Ebenezer Miller, a Friend, who resided at Greenwich, was a member of the Assembly this year, and doubtless procured this act. By this time fairs had become much less important than they had been, by the increase of regular retail stores, whose proprietors were anxious to get rid of the fairs. One of the provisions of the original concessions and agreements of the freeholders of West Jersey was that the streets in cities, towns, and villages should not be under one hundred feet wide. In pursuance of this, a street was laid out at Greenwich, from the wharf to where the Presbyterian church was afterwards built, of that width, but by whom is not known. It is quite probable that Fenwick himself visited the place in his barge, which he particularly mentions in his will; but it does not appear that he sold any lots there. His will provides "that Martha Smith, my Xtian friend, to have two lots of land at Cohansey, at the town intended on the river Cæsaria."*

* The following extract from an interesting account of the Ewing family, printed only for the use of the family, will give us a very good idea of the situation and habits of a well-to-do pious Presbyterian family in the county of Cumberland, about the middle of the eighteenth century. It is a part of the biography of the wife of Maskell Ewing, who married Mary Pagett, in 1743.

"His wife was a woman of plain manners, though lady-like, and very sensible. She was remarkable for her powers as a housekeeper. With the exception of her husband's Sunday-coat, which was the one that had served at his wedding, and which lasted for a good part of after life, she had on hand the making of his and their children's garments from the flax and the wool. All the bedding and house linen must be made, and geese kept to find materials for beds; some thousand weight of cheese to be prepared annually for market; poultry and calves to be raised; gardening to be done; the work of butchering-time to be attended to (this included the putting up of pork and salt meat to last the whole year, besides sausages for winter, and the making of candles); herbs to be gathered and dried, and

Penn and the executors of Fenwick made several conveyances of sixteen acre lots on the east side of the street; one to Mark Reeve, describes him as of Cæsaria River, and is dated August 9, 1686. It contains the lot at the corner near the wharf, on which he had built a house. In December of the same year Reeve, in consideration of £80, conveyed it to Joseph Browne, late of Phila- delphia, "reserving to himself and his heirs a free egress and re- gress to and from a certain piece of ground, containing 24 square feet, where the said Mark Reeve's wife lies buried." Browne con- veyed it to Chalkley, a Friend, in 1738, and he to John Butler. Butler conveyed it to Thomas Mulford, and he to William Conover, who conveyed it to John Sheppard, December 16, 1760, in whose family it has remained ever since. No survey under the proprie- tors appears to have been recorded for this lot. Chalkley, in 1739, laid a survey on half an acre adjoining it, including the wharf, and in 1743 another for 15½ acres, thus making up a sixteen acre lot.

One Zachariah Barrow possessed a farm held under Fenwick con- siderably further north, on the east side of the street, above the Friends' school-house, and by his will made in 1725 devised it " for the benefit of a free school for the town of Greenwich forever." In 1749, just after Cumberland County was established, to perfect the title—no survey having been before recorded—Ebenezer Miller pro- cured a survey to be duly laid on this farm to himself and two others, attorneys duly constituted by the *town* of Greenwich, and they exe- cuted a conveyance to David Sheppard, subject to a yearly rent of thirteen pounds, for the use of a free school to the inhabitants of the town of Greenwich, within certain bounds set forth in the deed. From this and other circumstances, it is known that Greenwich was made a township at an early day, and probably with the bounda-

ointments compounded ; besides all the ordinary house-work of washing, ironing, patching, darning, knitting, scrubbing, baking, cooking, and many other avoca- tions, which a farmer's wife now-a-days would be apt to think entirely out of her line. And all this without any ' help,' other than that afforded by her own little daughters, as they became able ; and for the first twenty-two years, with a baby always to be nursed. This afforded no time for any reading but the best ; but many a good book she contrived to read by laying it on her lap, whilst her hands plied the knitting-needles, or to hear read by the husband or one of the children, while she and the rest spent the evening in sewing. On the Sabbath, a folio Flavel, the Institutes of Calvin, and, above all, the Bible, were the treasures in which her soul delighted."

ries contained in the deed. The act establishing the county divides
it into six townships, the bounds of Greenwich containing considerably more territory than is described in the deed. In New England what we call townships are usually called towns. The reserved
rent continues to be paid, and by a decree of the Court of Chancery,
to and for the benefit of the public schools within the bounds of
the town, as described in the deed.

Fenwick's will, before quoted, mentions a creek called Bacon's
Creek. There is still extant a deed from two Indians to John
Nicholls of Nicholls Hartford, near Cohansey, dated 25th of 4th
month (June of the old style), 1683, whereby, in consideration of
one blanket, one double handful of powder, two bars of lead, three
pennyworths of paint, one hoe, one axe, one looking-glass, one pair
of scissors, one shirt, and one breech cloth, they sell and convey to
him a parcel of land containing, by estimation, one hundred acres,
beginning at a tree near the creek called the Great Tree Creek, and
bounding on Cohansey River and land of Henry Jennings, George
Hazlewood, and Samuel Bacon, who are believed to have been of
the early Baptist settlers. This deed was approved by Richard
Grey and James Nevill, in accordance with a law passed the same
year, which forbade the purchase of land from Indians without
their sanction. A somewhat similar deed is in the possession of
the Bacon family. Whether a title was also obtained by survey
under the proprietors is unknown. Unless there was, the legal
title of the present possessors rests upon the possession, and not
upon the Indian deeds.

Before the Revolutionary War it can hardly be said that there
were any towns in the county. Greenwich was the place of most
business up to the beginning of the present century. The stores
there contained the largest assortment of goods. A young lady
who visited Bridgeton in 1786, mentions, in a journal which has
been preserved, going to Greenwich " to get her broken watch crys-
tal replaced, but the man had not received any from Philadelphia
as he expected." She mentions going to Wood and Sheppard's
store to get a few trifles. They transacted so large a business as
to make it worth while to have bonds printed payable to them.
The river forming an excellent harbor, vessels traded direct to the
West Indies and other places ; but as New York overshadowed
Perth Amboy, so Philadelphia overshadowed Greenwich or Cohansie. There was a regular ferry kept up over the river, and much

intercourse between Fairfield and Greenwich. In 1767, after John Sheppard came there, a law was passed establishing the ferry, and in pursuance of its provisions, he bound himself to keep good and sufficient boats, fit for ferrying travellers and carriages for 999 years, and to keep and amend the roads, and bound his property to make good his agreement. About 1810, and again in 1820, efforts were made to have a draw-bridge built at the expense of the county; but this project was strenuously resisted by those living on the river above, and being defeated, caused much rejoicing. For several years a horse-boat was in constant use; but as other towns grew, and capital increased, Greenwich lost its relative importance, and the ferry had but little business, so that in 1838 Mr. Sheppard, in consideration of paying $300, was released from his engagement. Like other parts of the county, it has since greatly improved, but it is now only the depot of a rich agricultural region in its immediate neighborhood.*

Those familiar with the history of the English colonies in North America, will remember that it was the persistence of the British government in taxing the people, without allowing them to be represented in Parliament, that brought on the Revolution, and hastened their Independence. In 1773, all those taxes were repealed but the duty on tea, which our forefathers not only resolved not to use, but which they would not suffer to be landed and offered for sale. The East India Company, which then had the monopoly of this commodity, was encouraged to send it to this country, and was allowed a drawback of all the duties paid in England, it being supposed that the cheapness of the article would tempt our people to purchase largely. Cargoes were sent to all the large seaports; but at some places the tea was not permitted to be landed, and at others it was stored, but not allowed to be sold. In December, a party disguised as Indians boarded one of the ships in Boston harbor, and threw the tea into the water.

A brig called the Greyhound, bound to Philadelphia, with a cargo of tea, the captain of which was afraid to proceed to his place of destination, in the summer of 1774 came into the Cohansey, landed his tea, and had it stored in the cellar of a house standing in front of the then open market-square. This house is not now standing, and the market-square has been inclosed as private pro-

---

* When not otherwise stated, the time referred to as "now" is the year 1865.

perty. Imitating the example of the Bostonians, a company of
near forty men was organized, with the concurrence of the committee of safety of the county, of which Jonathan Elmer, the royal
sheriff, was an active member, who disguised themselves as Indians,
and on the night of November 22, 1774, broke into the store-house,
took out the boxes of tea, and burned them in a neighboring field.
The writer remembers to have known in his boyhood one of the
party, a man named Stacks, who, it was said, tied strings round his
pantaloons at his ankles, and stuffed them with tea, which he carried home to his family, and thus got the name of Tea-Stacks.

The owners of the tea commenced actions of trespass against
such of the disguised Indians as they thought they could identify,
in the Supreme Court of the State, Joseph Reed of Philadelphia,
and Mr. Petit of Burlington, being their lawyers. Money for the
defence was raised by subscription, and Joseph Bloomfield, then
residing at Bridgeton, George Read of New Castle, Elias Boudinot
of Elizabethtown, and Jonathan D. Serjeant of Philadelphia, all
eminent counsellors, were employed on behalf of the defendants.
No trial, however, ever took place. The plaintiffs were ruled to
enter security for the costs, which being neglected, a judgment of
non pros was entered at May Term, 1776, but at the succeeding
term security was filed, and the non pros set aside. The new
constitution of the State, adopted in July, having displaced the
Royal Judges, and their places being filled in the succeeding winter with Whigs, the actions were dropped, and no further proceedings took place on either side.

Ebenezer Elmer, who was one of the Indians, enters in a journal
he kept during the year 1775, under the date "Die Jovis 25 mo"
(Thursday, May 25, 1775), "Came up to Bridge (from his nephew
Daniel Elmer's, who lived at Cedarville) just before court, being
Supreme Court. Judge Smith gave very large charge to the grand
jury concerning the times, and the burning of the tea the fall
before, but the jury came in without doing anything, and the court
broke up." Under the date of September 7, he enters, "Expected
as Sheriff Bowen had got a jury of Tories, we should be indicted
for burning the tea and taking Wheaton, but they could not make
it out." Wheaton had been arrested by order of the committee of
safety, as a dangerous Tory, but, nothing appearing against him,
had been discharged. The grand jury, to whom he complained,
did make a presentment against the journalist and others, for an

assault and battery, and false imprisonment, which is now on file, but the court did not think proper to order a formal indictment to be presented, and nothing was done.

The Judge Smyth mentioned in the journal was Chief Justice Frederick Smyth, the last of the Royal judges who presided in the Oyer and Terminer of this county. His charge fell on very dull ears, the Whig sheriff, who knew all about the tea burning, having taken care to summon a Whig jury, the foreman of which was his nephew, Daniel Elmer. Before the ensuing September term this Whig sheriff, who held his office at the pleasure of Governor Franklin, who was not superseded until arrested by order of the Provincial Congress of New Jersey in the following June, was displaced, and David Bowen, who was supposed to be more loyal, was appointed in his place. He held the office of sheriff a little more than a year, being superseded in the fall of 1776 by Joel Fithian, who was elected pursuant to the new constitution.

The place now called Roadstown, surrounded by a fertile region, was settled at an early date, and until Cohansey Bridge was established as the county town, was the place next in importance to New England town, and Greenwich. It is called Kingstown in an old mortgage on record, but if it was ever generally known by that name, which is doubtful, that designation was wiped out by the Declaration of Independence. Prior to, and for some time after the Revolution, it was called Sayre's Cross Roads, Ananias Sayre, originally from Fairfield, who was a prominent citizen, and at one time sheriff, having settled there, and built the house at the northwest corner of the cross roads.

The first proprietors of the land within the bounds of what is now Cumberland, were principally, but not exclusively, Friends. But few of the actual settlers were Friends, that people being principally confined to Greenwich, and at a later day a few on Maurice River. Richard Hancock, who was Fenwick's first Surveyor General, after his falling out with him came to the place now called Bridgeton, and before 1686 erected a saw-mill on the stream then and since called Mill Creek, at the place where Pine Street now crosses the dam, then first made to form the pond. The low ground adjoining this creek was then covered with cedar trees, and pine and other large trees covered the hills. What title Hancock had to the land does not appear. It was included within the 11,000 acre survey, about this time located for the West Jersey

Society, formed by several large proprietors living partly in London and partly in the province. Probably he held under them. It does not appear that he ever lived here, his residence being at the place in Salem County named after him, Hancock's Bridge, where there still remain some of his descendants. Thomas says, "a goodly store of lumber went out of the Cohansey to Philadelphia."

It was an early regulation that surveys should not extend on both sides of navigable streams. Surveyors, of whom John Worlidge was one, are said to have come from Burlington in a boat. The rights west of the Cohansey seem all to have been purchased of Fenwick or his executors. Most of the land was covered by surveys before 1700. James Wasse, Joshua Barkstead, R. Hutchinson, George Hazlewood, John Budd, Cornelius Mason, and Edmund Gibbon made large surveys, which extended nearly from the Cohansey to the Salem line.

Edmund Gibbon, an English merchant residing in New York, in the year 1677, to secure a debt due to him by Edward Duke and Thomas Duke, took from them a conveyance of 6000 acres of land in West Jersey which had been conveyed to them by Fenwick in England. Gibbon, by virtue of this deed, had a tract of 5500 acres surveyed for him by Richard Hancock in 1682. It was resurveyed by Benj. Acton in 1703, and included within its bounds Roadstown, the east line running between the present Baptist meeting-house and the cross-roads, and extending southward to Pine Mount Branch, and westward to the Delaware. He devised this tract to his grandson Edmund, who devised it to Francis Gibbon of Bennensdere, England. In 1700 Francis devised it to his two kinsmen, Leonard and Nicholas Gibbon, of Gravesend in Kent, described as "all that part of lands called Mount Gibbon, upon the branches of unknown creek, near Cohansey in West New Jersey," provided they go and settle upon it. They both came over and erected the mill formerly owned by Richard Seeley, who was a descendant of Nicholas, and now by his daughter, the property having continued in the family to this time. This was probably the first mill erected for grinding grain, unless the tide mill, which was situate on the stream a little east of Greenwich Street, and has been many years gone, preceded it. A fulling mill was erected at an early day on Pine Mount (as Mount Gibbon is now called) Run. The mills of John S. Wood and of Benjamin Shep-

pard are also of old date.   Wood's Mill was for a long time owned
by John Brick, the tradition being that he also owned large tracts
in Lower Pittsgrove, and that through his influence the line between
Cumberland and Salem was so run as to leave them in the latter
county.   Leonard and Nicholas Gibbon divided their tract in 1730,
Nicholas taking the southern part, including the mill, and 2000
acres of land.   Nicholas built a good brick house in the town of
Greenwich, where he resided until 1740, when he removed to
Salem.   Leonard built a stone house about two miles north of
Greenwich.   Both these buildings remain, but have long since
gone out of the family, of whom there are still very respectable
descendants, residing principally in Salem.

On the east side of the Cohansey a large tract of 11,000 acres
was surveyed by Worlidge and Budd for the West Jersey Society
in 1686, and re-surveyed and recorded in 1716.   East of that tract
a large survey was made for the heirs of Penn, which extended to
Maurice River.   On the west side of that river, and bounding on
the Delaware, a large survey was made for Wasse.   In 1691 a
large survey was laid on the east side of Maurice River for Thomas
Byerly.   Indeed, it may be safely said that four-fifths of the land
included in Cumberland County was covered by surveys before
1700.

Surveys for Helby and John Bellers, creditors of Billing, living
in England, covered most of Fairfield.   The Helby surveys were
sold out to settlers at an early day, but the Bellers title was the
occasion of much difficulty.   It extended from Mill Creek, at
Fairton, to the Tweed or Back Creek.   His agent, Thomas Budd,
had a power of attorney to sell 400 acres, which he deeded to
Ephriam Seeley.*   But he made leases to the Connecticut settlers,

* Thomas Budd became a Friend in England, came over to Burlington in West
Jersey, in 1678, and held several important offices in the province.   In 1681, he
was chosen, by the Assembly, a commissioner for "settling and regulation of
lands, and was afterward a member of the Assembly.   In 1684 he went to England, and there published a pamphlet entitled, "Good order established in Pennsylvania and New Jersey, in America, being a true account of the country."
Probably he had not at this time visited South Jersey, as he confines his description to the parts in the vicinity of Burlington.   This pamphlet has been recently
published with very copious and interesting historical notes, by Edward Armstrong, Esq., of Philadelphia.

Budd appears to have returned to Burlington the same year, and soon afterwards removed to Philadelphia, where he owned considerable property, took an

reserving small quit-rents, and entered into bonds that a good title should be made, or their improvements paid for. Under these leases most of the tract was parcelled out to the settlers, and the land improved. But Bellers appears to have been ambitious of being lord of a manor in America, and upon his death in 1724 entailed this property so that it could not be sold. The Rev. Daniel Elmer procured the semblance of a title to the 400 acres of Seeley's heirs, and in 1745 located part of this right so as to include the farm on which he resided and had built himself a house, and the adjoining meeting-house lot and burial ground lying on Cohansey River, below Fairton. About the same time he and his son Daniel, who was a surveyor, laid out a town, which was never built, on the bank of the river, extending eastwardly so as to include part of the present sight of Fairton, which it was proposed to call Fairfield. Could the title have been secured, it would probably have become an important town and the county seat. In 1750 the settlers sent over Capt. Thomas Harris to England with money to purchase the Bellers title; but, not succeeding, he laid out the money in Bibles, Watts' Psalms and Hymns, then just coming into use, a folio edition of Flavel, and pewter dishes, which were distributed among those willing to take them. The pewter dishes took the place of wooden trenchers for those able to indulge in such a luxury. Some of them and some copies of Flavel still remain.

It was not until about 1811 that this Bellers title was extinguished. When about ten years before this time the late Benjamin Chew, of Philadelphia, became the agent of the English proprietors, the occupants refused to purchase, and resisted the surveyors who attempted to run out the tract, and cut off the tail of the agent's horse. Suits were brought, and the Supreme Court of this State made a special order, requiring the sheriff to call out the *posse comitatus* and protect the surveyors, who pointed out the land to a jury of view. One case was tried, and a verdict rendered for the plaintiff. A compromise then took place, by which three persons from the adjoining counties were selected to determine how much the occupants should pay. They awarded two dollars

active part in disputes that arose among the Friends, and died in the year 1698. His descendants, and those of his brother William, who resided in Burlington County and was an Episcopalian, are numerous and very respectable, in Pennsylvania and New Jersey.

and fifty cents per acre, and seventy-five cents per acre for the costs, which was eventually paid, and deeds made to each occupant. A small part of it remains nominally in Chew's heirs.

A similar difficulty occurred when the proprietors of the Penn tract commenced selling. A gentleman now living remembers when, about the year 1804, the squatters thereon threatened to hang the agent, who had some difficulty in effecting his escape, which he was enabled to do by the swiftness of his horse that carried him safely over Maurice River bridge at Millville before his pursuers could overtake him.

A map annexed to Thomas's description of Pennsylvania and West Jersey, before referred to, contains on it the names of two towns, viz: Dorchester, on the east side of Maurice River, and Antioch, on the south side of Cohansey, the only towns within the bounds of Cumberland which are named. Dorchester was surveyed and returned as a town plat of 2500 acres, and although no town was built until after 1800, it retains the name. Antioch was probably surveyed in a similar manner, but never recorded, unless, as is most probable, the map places it on the wrong side of the river. The original map of Hancock's survey for Gibbon, refers to the boundaries of Antioch or Greenwich town. No town called Antioch ever existed in the county.

The Connecticut immigrants called the place most thickly settled New England Town, by which name, or that of New England Town Cross-roads, it was long known. The first road from Salem to Maurice River was laid out in 1705, through Greenwich, crossing the river there, and then along by the meeting-house at New England Town, up to the neighborhood of the present Fairton, and then through the woods towards Maurice River, without stating precisely where it was to go or where to end. The road from New England Town to Burlington—the seat of government of West Jersey—was no doubt the first road used in the county. It passed over the north branch of the Cohansey, called Mill Creek, at a place where the mill was first erected, somewhat below the present mill-dam, and then along the Indian path about a mile east of Bridgeton, through the Indian fields, passing by the Pine Tavern, then over to the road from Salem, near the present Clarksboro in Gloucester County, then through Woodbury and Haddonfield. The bridge and road at Carpenter's Landing were not made until the forepart of the present century.

Fairton was not so called until the post-office was established, about the year 1812. It was previously called by the nickname Bumbridge, a name said to have originated from the circumstance that a constable—then often called a Bum-bailiff, which is a corruption of the word bound bailiff, that is, a bailiff bound with a security—in attempting to arrest a person, fell into the water, owing to some defect in the bridge over Rattlesnake Run, and thus occasioned the bridge to be rebuilt, and to acquire a name. For many years the road over this run crossed considerably above where the bridge was made. When the country was first settled, what is now called Mill Creek, at Fairton, was known as the north branch of the Cohansey.

Cedarville became a place of some local importance directly after the Revolution, but was not known by this name until the post-office was established. It was settled at an early period; but when the mill was erected is not known.

Gouldtown—partly in the northern part of Fairfield, and partly in Bridgeton townships—although never more than a settlement of mulattoes principally bearing the names of Gould and Pierce, scattered over a considerable territory, is of quite ancient date. The tradition is that they are descendants of Fenwick. His will contains the following clause: "Item, I do except against Elizabeth Adams (who was a granddaughter), of having any the least part of my estate, unless the Lord open her eyes to see her abominable transgression against him, me, and her good father, by giving her true repentance, and forsaking that Black that hath been the ruin of her, and becoming penitent for her sins; upon that condition only I do will and require my executors to settle five hundred acres of land upon her."

3

CHAPTER II.

GOVERNMENT AND OFFICERS.

THE government of New Jersey was at first assumed by the proprietors. After the partition into two provinces, West Jersey was intended to be divided into Tenths, fronting on the Delaware, but only three or four were defined, and these were soon superseded by regular counties; and indeed the tenths seem to have been designed rather for the purpose of apportioning the land among the different proprietors than for the purposes of government. The General Assembly which convened at Burlington May 2, 1682, appointed Justices, Sheriff, and Clerk for the jurisdiction of Burlington, and others for the jurisdiction of Salem, and Courts of Sessions were directed to be held four times a year at each place. No definite limits were assigned to these "jurisdictions," it being probably the design that the officers designated should have power to act in all parts of the province. In 1683 the members of Assembly were elected separately, in the First, Second, and Salem Tenths, and the justices and sheriffs appointed as before. In 1685 an act was passed establishing the county of Cape May, and bounding it on the west by Maurice River, authorizing justices to try causes under forty shillings, but other actions, civil and criminal, to be tried in Salem County. This act states that the province had been formerly divided into three counties, but no act for that purpose is in print; indeed none of the acts passed in West Jersey were printed until such as could be found were published by Leaming and Spicer in 1750.

In 1692 the boundary between Gloucester and Burlington was altered, but the next year the act was repealed. In 1693 Cape May was authorized to have a county court. In 1694 the boundaries of Burlington and Gloucester were established; and it was enacted that the jurisdiction of Salem court should extend from Berkeley River (now called Oldman's Creek) on the north, to the Tweed (now called Back Creek) on the south. The district between the Tweed and Maurice River was not included in any county.

To remedy this it was enacted in 1700 that all persons inhabiting on the river Tweed, and all settlements below, unto the bounds of the county of Cape May, should from thenceforth be annexed to, and be subject to the jurisdiction of the court and county of Salem. After the union of the two provinces by the surrender of the government to Queen Anne, an act was passed in January, 1709–10, still partly in force, ascertaining the boundaries of all the counties in the province of New Jersey, which reduced Cape May to its present dimensions, and extended Salem to the western boundary of Cape May.

The act establishing the county provided that whenever the freeholders and justices should judge it necessary to build a courthouse and jail, an election to determine the place should be held at John Butler's in the town of Greenwich, on a day to be fixed by three of the justices, one of whom should be of the quorum. It being the prerogative of the governor to appoint the time of holding the courts, he issued an ordinance directing them to be held in the meantime at Greenwich, four times a year. A small wooden jail was built in that place, and the courts were held for a time in the Presbyterian meeting-house and the tavern.

An election was held in 1748, by which a majority of those who voted declared in favor of Cohansey Bridge, and to this place the court held in December of that year adjourned. When the justices and freeholders met there in July of that year, the minutes state that "it was proposed to raise money for a jail and courthouse; but the major part of the justices and freeholders present were not so disposed—as to the location of the place where the said jail and court-house shall be built, and thought proper to settle the point first, before they consent to raise money for that purpose; but in order to settle the affair of the election, there was a motion made for to examine the voters by purging them by their respective oaths and affirmations, but the freeholders of the south side of Cohansey refused to comply with said offer. There being no business to do, the meeting adjourned." In 1749, a dispute arose as to the election of the freeholders in Hopewell. In 1750, there was a full board, and it was agreed that "there shall be a deed drafted and delivered to Richard Wood and Ebenezer Miller to peruse, and upon their approbation, then they, or more of the justices, are to summons magistrates and freeholders to proceed upon raising money to build a court-house and jail." In 1751 and 1752, money was ordered raised. Wood and Miller both lived at Greenwich, but the latter had become largely interested in the property at Cohansey Bridge, and joined the south siders. The lot was a part of his survey, including the present jail, and extending across Broad Street; and a question being raised about the title, a number of the most prominent freeholders on the south side, as the eastern part of the county was then designated, including Miller, joined in a bond in the penal sum of two hundred pounds, to several of the freeholders at Greenwich, to guarantee the title.

The bridge over the Cohansey was built, resting on cribs sunk in the water, as early as 1716, it being referred to in a survey of that date; but whether it was then passable for carriages may be doubted, as probably there were no four-wheeled wagons at that time, or for long afterwards, in the county. Lumber was floated by water, or, when necessary, drawn for short distances on sleds. A very old man, named Murray, said forty years ago, that he remembered when there was a small store on the west side of the river, near the water, and a bridge for foot-passengers only. When the tide was out the stream was fordable, and an old survey made in 1686, mentions the going-over place to Richard Hancock's mill. A road for use when the tide was in used to cross the stream about half way up the present pond, the marks of which were not long since visible.

When the courts were first held at Cohansey Bridge, it is supposed there were no more than eight or ten houses in the immediate vicinity. The road from Salem passed a little south of where the old Presbyterian Church stands, at the west end of the town, and entering Broad Street, passed down the same to near the corner of Franklin Street, then came down the hill a northeast course, past the corner of the large stone house, which stands a little back from and west of Atlantic Street, and thence to the foot of the bridge; passing the bridge, it ran nearly the present course of Commerce Street to near Pearl Street, and then a northeast course, a little south of the stone Presbyterian church, and so on through what was then woodland, to near the corner of East Avenue and Irving Street, and thence through the Indian Fields, over the Beaver Dam at Lebanon Run to Maurice River. A house stood on the brow of the hill, a little west of the run that crosses this road, next east of the railroad station, where there was at one time a tavern; and between that and the railroad, about opposite to East Avenue, there was a graveyard. At or near the place where Pearl Street crosses Commerce Street, the roads forked, one branch running northwardly to Deerfield. It was necessary to go thus far east of the bridge before turning northwardly, to avoid going up Laurel Hill, then impassable, without the outlay of much labor and expense. At the Indian Fields the road then and now running north and south, originally an Indian path, became the king's highway from Fairfield to the seat of government at Burlington. It is the most ancient road in the county, and is even yet known to the old inhabitants as the old Burlington road, and in 1769 was laid out as a public road, four rods wide.

The mill-pond, now owned by Jonathan Elmer, was in 1748 owned by Ephraim Seeley, commonly called Col. Seeley. The mill stood in the low ground back of the house occupied by Mrs. Du Bois, and the dam crossed above from the hill diagonally to the point where there is now a brick kiln. The old mansion house stood on the hill northeast of Mrs. Du Bois, near the pond, and the road from the bridge over Cohansey, to the house and mill, ran about where the back part of Jonathan Elmer's house now stands. There was a bridge across the saw-mill pond, back of the Methodist meeting-house lot, over which the road to Fairfield passed, which was laid out as a public road in 1763. This road crossed Mill Creek near Fairton, at Joseph Ogden's mill-dam, which was lower down the stream than the present dam.

Seeley's mill was erected at an early date, but when or by whom has not been ascertained; but the writer recollects that fifty years ago the remains of an old fulling mill were visible near the middle of the dam, and he has heard that Col. Seeley's wife was accustomed, in her youth, to ride on horseback as far as Cape May, carrying with her fulled cloth, and returning with a horse load of cloth to be dressed. At that time nearly all the clothing and the bedding used by the people was spun in the family, and often woven there also, or by persons who followed the business. The straight road to Millville, now a turnpike, was laid out in 1805, commencing at the bridge; and in 1809 Jeremiah Buck erected the dam and flour and saw-mills now standing, and it may be mentioned that Mr. French, the millwright, from near Bordentown, lost his life at the raising of the saw-mill, having been crushed by falling timbers.

Besides Seeley's mill and house, the old Hancock mill still remained in 1748. It was removed to a site just below the present stone bridge, and the existing race-way cut in 1772. This saw-mill and the pond above, upon which the writer has often skated, remained until 1809, when Mr. Buck lowered the race-way and pond, as low as the tide would permit, to obtain a better head and fall at his mills above, and the mill was taken down. There was a house near this saw-mill on the northwest side of Pine Street, long owned and occupied by Col. Enos Seeley, a relative of Col. Ephraim, and grandfather of the late Governor E. P. Seeley, which probably stood there in 1748. It was long occupied by the widow Jay, and was taken down about 20 years ago. Col. Enos Seeley, in 1772, owned all the property where the glass-houses now are, his northern line being about where Jefferson Street now is, adjoining Alexander Moore's line, and included a house standing where Mrs. Buck's house now is, fronting Laurel Street. This house was there in 1748, and upon the creek, an old wharf, the first erected, called in old writings Smith's Wharf, used, probably, in connection with Hancock's mill. At this time the dam leading to the stone bridge was not made, but the tide flowed up the old channel of Mill Creek to the neighborhood of the mill. Col. Enos Seeley put up the dam about the year 1774.

Nearly opposite Col. Seeley's house, now Mrs. Buck's, was a good house facing the south, in which a store was afterwards kept by Mr. Boyd and his widow. There were also two or three houses nearly opposite, on the east side of Laurel Street. These are believed to have been all the houses on the east side of the river, until Alexander Moore built his dwelling-house, on the north side of Commerce Street, about half way between the hotel and the bridge. His store-house of cedar logs stood where Potter's store-house now is. Judge White told the writer he took it down, and found in it an old horn book; that is to say, a printed card containing the alphabet and a short lesson in spelling, which was pasted to a piece of board and covered with a horn pressed flat and scraped thin, so as to be transparent enough to leave the lessons visible to the urchins who were to learn them, and thus protecting them from being defaced. Such books, made however after different patterns, were in common use a century ago. Moore is believed to have settled here between 1730 and 1740. He married a descendant of Mark Reeve. Most of the site of East Bridgeton, north of Commerce Street, was an open woods in 1748, and so continued until after the Revolutionary War.

On the west side of the river, a good two-storied house, with what was commonly called a hip roof, stood a little south of Commerce Street, facing the east, the back part of which was about where the east side of Atlantic Street now is, in front of which was the road which ran a southwest course up the hill, having a south fork running down the river, and between the road and river was a garden. This was built about 1725, by Silas Parvin, and was for several years licensed as a tavern, and stood there about one hundred years, when it was removed by the late Smith Bowen. South of this and near the river, a little north of Broad Street, at the place now owned by James B. Potter and used as a ship-yard, stood a good house fronting the north, owned in 1748 by Capt. Elias Cotting. It was afterwards for many years owned and occupied by Enoch Boon, and has been taken down some twenty years and more. When first erected it was a mansion of considerable pretension. Another house stood a little back of where the court-house now stands, on a road early used to the marshes, upon which the early settlers depended almost exclusively for hay, and belonged to one Jeremiah Sayre, cordwainer. Neither Broad Street nor Commerce Street was opened up the hill until many years after this period. These three dwelling-houses and a small store-house of cedar logs standing north of Parvin's house and a farm-house on the property above Muddy Branch, were all the buildings on the west side of Cohansey Bridge.

The Court was first held at Isaac Smith's who probably kept a tavern in the Parvin house, in February 1748, old style, and generally met at eight o'clock in the morning. Cotting was commissioned by the Governor as clerk, at first to hold during the pleasure of the Governor, but in 1755 he presented a commission to hold during good behavior, which continued the mode until 1776. He died in 1757, and was succeeded by Daniel Elmer, who died in 1761, and was succeeded by Maskel Ewing, who, having taken an oath of allegiance to the king, declined to serve under the new government. In 1786 Jonathan Elmer presented a commission from Governor Livingston as clerk, and in the ensuing fall he was elected by the joint meeting for five years pursuant to the constitution; Alexander Moore and Ephraim Seeley appeared as judges. The September term does not appear to have been held. The terms were held four times in the year, and until 1752 the February term is always entered of the same year as the preceding December term, it thus appearing that the old style was changed that year. According to the old style, the year commenced on the feast of the conception of Mary or Lady day, March 25th, which still continues to be the customary day of commencing leases in this county, although in other parts of the State it is the first day of April according to the Pennsylvania usage, and in some places the first day of May agreeably to the New York usage.

Cohansey Bridge is mentioned in the minutes until 1765, when Bridgetown is first named. Constables for the town were first appointed by the court in 1768. It may be noticed that the whole region from the source of the river near Friesburgh, to its mouth at the Delaware Bay, was commonly called Cohansey, up to and even after the Revolution. It was common to write Fairfield in Cohansey, or Greenwich Cohansey. Upon the establishment of the Bank in 1816, its first president, Gen. Giles, had the name of the town printed Bridgeton on the notes, and this soon became the adopted name. Bridgetown, however, still remains the official name of the port, under the laws of the United States.

The following named persons have been the clerks, after those above named, from 1776 appointed by joint meeting for five years, vacancies filled by Governor, until 1846, and since by election in the county :—

James Giles,   appointed in   1789
Dr. Azel Pierson,   "   1804 died
Jonathan Holmes, by Governor 1812
Dr. Edo Ogden, appointed in 1813 died
Ebenezer Elmer, by Governor 1813
Ebenezer Seeley, appointed in 1814 died
Samuel Seeley,   "   1833

Josiah Fithian, appointed in 1838 died
Enos Seeley,   by Governor 1842
D. M. Woodruff, appointed in 1842
        "   elected   1847
Ephraim E. Sheppard, "   1852
Providence Ludlam,   "   1857
Theo. G. Compton,   "   1862

The following named persons have been surrogates, appointed until 1822 by the Governor to hold at his pleasure; then until 1846 by the joint meeting of the legislature, to hold for five years, vacancies happening being filled by the Governor to hold until the legislature met; since 1846 by election in the county:—

Elias Cotting, appointed 1748
Daniel Elmer,   "   1757
Maskel Ewing,   "   1761
Jonathan Elmer,   "   1776
George Burgin   "   1804 died 1810
Ebenezer Elmer   "   1810
Jonathan Elmer,   "   1812

Sam'l M. Shute, app'ted 1813
Timothy Elmer,   "   1815 died 1836
Wm. S. Bowen,   "   1836
H. R. Merseilles, "   1837
Joseph Moore, elected 1852
H. R. Merseilles,   "   1857 died
Alphonso Woodruff, "   1861

At a session of the Assembly in 1690, an act was passed "that the tract of land in Cohansey purchased by several people, lately inhabitants of Fairfield, in New England, be erected into a township." One of the vessels containing these immigrants came up the creek now called Back Creek, and gave it the name of the Tweed. Their tract was at the head of this stream, and between it and the Cohansey, which probably occasioned the extension of Salem County, so as to include them. The precise date of the arrival of these New Englanders is unknown, but it was probably from 1682 to 1690. The Bellers tract was first surveyed in 1686, and it was from Thomas Budd, agent of that proprietor, they leased. No records of the town-meetings—prior to the early part of the present century—are extant, but there can be no doubt that these inhabitants, isolated as they then were, instituted a local government sufficient for their immediate purposes, after the model of the towns of Connecticut—from which province most of these came—in which the affairs of church and state were curiously blended, with a most happy effect. Several of them—consisting of Congregationalists, or Presbyterians and Baptists—crossed the river to Greenwich, and were joined there by settlers from England, Scotland, and Ireland, mostly of the Presbyterian order.

It appears by the court records at Salem that at least as early as 1720 Fairfield and Greenwich were recognized as regular townships. The inhabitants in other neighborhoods, not considered as belonging to those townships, were provided with precinct officers appointed by the Court of Quarter Sessions. In 1709, the grand jury ordered a tax of 75 pounds to be levied, for county purposes, and appointed an assessor and collector for the north side of the Cohansey, and the same for the south side. In 1720, officers were first appointed for the precinct of Maurice River, and afterwards they were appointed in like manner yearly, until the county was organized. The Quarter Sessions in England were accustomed to appoint constables, where they were considered necessary, to prevent a failure of justice, and the same custom prevailed in New Jersey, except where townships were regularly organized and empowered to choose them.

Much inconvenience being experienced by the inhabitants living remote from Salem Town, several unsuccessful efforts were made to obtain a new county, which were rendered the more difficult by the desire of the royal governors to keep up the equality of representation in the Assembly, between East and West Jersey. In January, 1747–8, the attempt succeeded, but with the condition that members of Assembly should continue to be elected in conjunction with Salem. It was not until 1768 that two members were allowed to be chosen in Cumberland, which were balanced by two chosen in Morris County. It was not, however, until 1772 that writs were issued for a new election.

The act divided the new county into six townships, assigning to them their respective boundaries—three on the west, or north side of Cohansey, and three on the east, or south side. At least half the inhabitants then resided west of Cohansey, although the territory east of that river is about five times larger. Only Deerfield and a part of Fairfield contained more than a few settlers. Fairfield at first included all the present township of Downe. This township was set off by letters patent granted by Governor Franklin, in the year 1772, recorded in the Secretary of State's office at Trenton. This power was occasionally exercised by the governors of the province as a part of the royal prerogative, delegated to them by their commissions. His wife's maiden name was Elizabeth Downes, and the new township was named in compliment to her. It is spelled Downes in the record, but by a clerical or typographical error, the name was printed, in the law passed in 1798 incorporating the township, Downe, and has been so printed in all the laws since.

Some of the old surveys call for the line of the township of Pamphylia, at or near the place where the line between Fairfield and Deerfield was established; but this old Grecian name is retained only by the spring so called on the banks of the Cohansey, about a mile below the bridge. Maurice River contained originally all the large territory east of the river so called. Millville was set off from it, including parts of Deerfield and Fairfield, on the west of the river by a law passed in the year 1801. Bridgeton was set off from Deerfield by law, in 1845; and Cohansey from Hopewell by law, in 1848.

The legislature of the colony was convened, adjourned, and dissolved at the pleasure of the Governor and his Council, and the members of the Assembly were elected by virtue of writs under the great seal of the colony, directed to the sheriffs. By a law passed in 1725, the sheriff was required to give notice of the day and place of election, and then to proceed by reading his writ; and he was not to declare the choice by the view (that is, merely from a vote by holding up of hands), nor adjourn without the consent of the candidates; but if a poll was required, proceed from day to day, until all the electors present be polled; and he was required to appoint a clerk, who should set down the names of the electors, and the persons they voted for. There was, of course, but one place of election—generally the court-house in the county—and the election commonly closed the first day, but was occasionally kept open several days or even weeks. The voting was, of course, *viva voce*, ballots not being introduced until about 1790.

This power of the candidates to control the election, in some respects, gave rise to the system of making nominations in writing, which prevailed from 1790 until 1839, and was, it is supposed, peculiar to this State. At first the names of candidates were required to be posted up in some conspicuous place the first day; then they were required to be nominated on the election day before three o'clock, by some person entitled to vote; the name was then enrolled by the clerk, and fixed up in full view at the door of the house where the election was held. Elections being required to be held in each township in the year 1790, the clerk of the county was required to attend at the court-house on the first Monday in September, and there receive, from any person, entitled to vote, a list of the persons proposed as candidates, and the clerk then made a general list of all the candidates nominated, a certified copy of which was sent to each of the township clerks, and no person could be voted for unless he had been thus nominated. Of course, many were nominated who were not expected to be voted for, but occasionally the person who would have been preferred was found to have been omitted. After newspapers became common, it was customary to publish the list of nominations, often containing many names of low and vicious characters, nominated by way of joke by foolish persons, and the names of those who declined were so marked.

In the journal of Ebenezer Elmer, he enters under the date of September 21, 1775, " County met to choose two delegates and a county committee. Delegates chosen by poll, when Theophilus Elmer had a great majority, and next highest Esq. Jona. Ayres." Theophilus Elmer had been previously elected in 1772. To entitle a person to a seat in the Assembly at this time, he was required

to have 1000 acres of land in his own right, to be worth £500 of
real and personal estate. A voter must be a freeholder, and have
100 acres of land in his own right, or be worth £50 in real and personal estate. The members chosen for Salem and Cumberland in
1749 were William Hancock and John Brick. In 1751, William
Hancock and Richard Wood. In 1754, Hancock and Ebenezer
Miller. In 1761, the same. In 1769, Ebenezer Miller and Isaac
Sharp. In 1772, for Cumberland, John Sheppard and Theophilus
Elmer. Afterwards one member of Council, and three members
of Assembly, were chosen annually. For 1776, they were Theo-
philus Elmer, Council, Ephraim Harris, Jonathan Bowen, and John
Brick, Assembly. In 1778, Ephraim Harris, Council, Buck, Bowen,
and James Ewing, Assembly. In 1779, Buck, Council, Jas. Ewing,
Joel Fithian, and Timothy Elmer, Assembly. In 1780, Jonathan
Elmer, Council, same members of Assembly. In 1781, Samuel
Ogden, Council, Joshua Ewing, Joshua Brick, and Josiah Seeley,
Assembly. In 1782, Theophilus Elmer, Council, Joshua Ewing,
Ephraim Harris, Speaker, Jonathan Bowen, Assembly. Theophilus
Elmer was a member of the Council of Safety during most of the
Revolution.

The following persons, residing in the county, have been members of Congress :—

SENATE.—1789 to 1791, Jonathan Elmer; 1826 to 1827, when
he died, Ephraim Bateman.

HOUSE.—1776-7-81-82-83-87-88, Jonathan Elmer; 1801 to
1806, Ebenezer Elmer; 1815 to 1821, Ephraim Bateman; 1831 to
1835, Thomas Lee; 1843 to 1845, Lucius Q. C. Elmer; 1845 to
1849, James G. Hampton; 1859 to 1863, John T. Nixon.

The Constitution, adopted in 1776, instead of requiring every
voter to be worth fifty pounds of real and personal estate, required
only that he should be an inhabitant of the State, of full age, and
worth fifty pounds clear estate. The word inhabitant was probably adopted instead of citizen, under the impression that as a new
government was initiated it was proper to recognize all the inhabitants as citizens thereof. Under this broad provision, females and
colored persons were allowed to vote if worth the requisite sum,
and cases occurred when the voter presented himself or herself
with fifty pounds, $133 33 in hand in cash. No married females
voted, and few others. Very few colored persons were worth the
requisite sum. In 1807 an act of the legislature was passed, re-

citing that doubts had been raised, and great diversities of practice obtained throughout the State, in regard to the admission of aliens, females and persons of color, or negroes, to vote in elections, and also in regard to the mode of ascertaining the qualifications of voters in respect to estate, to remedy which it was provided that none but free white male citizens of the State should vote, and that every person who should have paid a tax, and whose name was enrolled on the tax list, should be adjudged to be worth fifty pounds. The late Dr. Lewis Condict, of Morristown, who recently died at a very advanced age, was at the time an active member of the Assembly, and had the credit of bringing forward this measure, which, however questionable as to its strict accordance with the Constitution, met the views of a great majority of the people of all parties, and continued the law until the adoption of the present Constitution, which contained substantially the same provisions. It was, however, occasionally decided by officers of the election that the law was unconstitutional and void; and it was under such a decision that at the contested election for the court-house, votes of aliens were admitted in one or more of the townships, and the same thing was done at a subsequent county and congregational election, which, with other circumstances, brought on what was called the broad seal war in 1837.

From 1809 to 1845 the polls were kept open two days, and the town meetings, which then and now fixed the place of holding the elections, were accustomed, in the larger townships, to order that they should be held on the first day at one place, and on the second at another, much to the convenience of the voters. It may indeed be doubted whether as many evils have not grown out of the change as have been cured. No careful observer can have failed to perceive that the practice of bribing voters, by means of direct payments of money, confined at first to a sufficient sum to defray the voter's expenses, but gradually enlarged until there are voters who are known regularly to sell their votes to the highest bidder, has greatly increased. Forty years ago a candidate for office was expected to remain quietly at home; now he would find favor with very few by such a course.

The county business was transacted by a board consisting of two freeholders elected in each township, as provided for in an act passed in 1714, and all the justices of the peace of the county, or any three of them, one whereof being of the quorum. All the justices for each county were generally included in one commission, as is the practice in England, and one or more were designated as of the quorum, without whose presence no business could be done. In case any town or precinct should neglect to elect freeholders, the justices were authorized to appoint them. The name precinct appears to have been applied to neighborhoods, without definite boundaries, not included within a defined township. The justices were appointed by the Governor and Council, until 1776, and held their offices at their pleasure. A book containing the proceedings of the freeholders and justices is still extant. The boards of freeholders were incorporated and organized, as they now exist, in 1798.

The following named persons have held the office of sheriff. Before the Revolution they were appointed by the Governor and Council, to hold for three years or during the pleasure of the Governor; and since they have been elected yearly, but can only hold the office three years in succession :—

Ananias Sayre,	appointed in	1747–8	William Rose,	elected	1810
Samuel Fithian,	"	1750–1	John Sibley,	"	1813
Ananias Sayre,	"	1754	Dan. Simpkins,	"	1816
Maskell Ewing,	"	1757	William R. Fithian,	"	1819
Silas Newcomb,	"	1760	John Lanning, jr.,	"	1822
Howel Powell,	"	1763	Robert S. Buck,	"	1825
Theophilus Elmer,	"	1766.	Josiah Shaw,	"	1828
Thomas Maskell,	"	1769	Daniel M. Woodruff,	"	1831
Jonathan Elmer,	"	1772	Cornelius Lupton,	"	1834
David Bowen,	"	1775	David Campbell,	"	1837
Joel Fithian,	elected	1776	Levi T. Davis,	"	1839
William Kelsay,	"	1779	Harris B. Mattison,	"	1842
Daniel Maskell,	"	1784	Cornelius Lupton,	"	1844
Joseph Buck,	"	1787	Stephen Murphy,	"	1845
David Potter,	"	1790	Theophilus E. Harris,	"	1848
Reuben Burgin,	"	1793	James Stiles,	"	1851
George Burgin,	"	1796	Nathaniel Stratton,	"	1854
Jeremiah Bennett, jr.,	"	1799	Jonathan Fithian,	"	1857
Enoch Burgin,	"	1802	Lewis H. Dowdney,	"	1860
Timothy Elmer,	"	1805	Charles L. Watson,	"	1863
John Buck,	"	1808	Samuel Peacock.	"	1866

The first court-house and jail were small wooden buildings. In 1753 money was raised for building a jail, to be of brick, 34 by 24 feet, and also stocks and a pillory. In 1755 an account was allowed for digging a dungeon and for stone. Much complaint was made of the insecurity of the jail, so that in 1757 a petition was sent to the Chief Justice, urging him to solicit the Governor to appoint a special oyer and terminer, the messenger being required to go and return in five days. Jeremiah Buck was the messenger, who of course made the journey on horseback, and was paid for six days at five shillings per day.

In 1759 it was agreed to build a new court-house of brick, two stories, 34 by 24 feet, with a cupola; Ebenezer Miller, David Sheppard, and Samuel Fithian, all north-siders, were the committee. During the years 1760 and '61 this house was built, and stood in the middle of what is now Broad Street, opposite the dwelling-house of the jail keeper, and continued to be used until 1846, about eighty-four years. The bell was purchased by subscription, and for many years the house was used on Sundays and other days for religious meetings. Evening meetings continued to be held in it until but a few years before it was taken down. The jail yard was inclosed with the walls in 1765. In 1767 the townships of Greenwich and Stow Creek were authorized to have each a pair of stocks. In 1775 a fence was ordered to be put up at the west end of the court-house, and in 1777 one was ordered at the east end, to prevent ball being played there. In 1790 the present jail was built on the site of the old one. About 1809 a market house was built by private subscription, and by consent of the freeholders, at the west end of the court-house. It was never much used, except on training or other public days. The pump in the street was put there by private subscription, aided by a donation from the freeholders, the main purpose being to reach the lower springs, which only, in that vicinity, furnish good water. A liberty pole was put up by the Democrats about 1802, near where the flag-staff now stands, which remained for many years, and was sometimes degraded to a whipping-post, when that punishment was in vogue.[1] Up to 1815 the clerks and surrogates kept their books and papers where they happened to live, which was not always in Bridgeton. In that year the fire-proof offices on Commerce Street were erected, being originally a low one-story building, more like a blacksmith shop than public offices.

About the year 1830 there began to be a desire to have a better

[1] Since this was written the old jail has been taken down. It stood a little south of the existing brick sheriff's house and jail, erected in 1867. The street has been newly graded, and the flagstaff and pump have disappeared.

court-house; and in 1836 the lot on which it now stands was purchased, there being then standing on it a large three-storied house,
built and used for many years as a tavern, but, after 1810, occupied by Rev. Jonathan Freeman. This produced an agitation to
remove the county seat to Millville; and, in pursuance of a special
law, an election was held July 25 and 26, 1837, to determine the
question. After a warm contest, the result was 1284 votes for
Bridgeton, 1059 for Millville, and 214 for Fairton. When the
battle began to wax warm, and especially when it was found that
the jealousy of some persons in Fairton would induce them to
throw away their votes on that place, the people of Bridgeton were
frightened, and issued hand-bills to the purport that the expense
of a new building was useless, the old one being good enough.
The result was a long contest in the Board of Freeholders, there
being eight townships, four of which voted steadily against a new
house, and the other four not only voted for a new house, but
against selling the lot lately purchased. In 1843, by the efforts of
two or three individuals, a law was passed establishing a new
township at Shiloh, under the plea that it was a political manœuvre,
and so skilfully was the matter managed, that the real object was
not suspected until it was too late. When the Board of Freeholders
met, five townships voted to build a new court-house, thus over-
powering the four who were opposed to it. Finding themselves
thus caught, the freeholders of the four eastern townships cordially
united in building the present house, which was finished and first
occupied in 1845. The next year the fire-proof offices on Commerce Street were raised and much improved. The existing fire-
proof record rooms in the rear were added in 1859. All disputes
about the court-house and offices being thus happily ended, the
inhabitants of the other parts of the county no longer opposed new
townships being created on both sides of the river, which were
found important for the convenience of a rapidly growing town.
The new township at Shiloh, called Columbia, existed but one
year.

The persons of all descriptions inhabiting Cumberland County
when it was set off, did not number 3000. In 1745, there were
only 6847 inhabitants in the bounds of Salem, as it then existed.
An act of Assembly passed in 1752, affords some means of ascertaining the relative positions of the two counties after the separa-
tion. Of the sum of fifteen hundred and thirty pounds required

for the state tax, the sum of one hundred and six pounds was required to be raised by Salem, and a very little more than half as much, namely, fifty-four pounds by Cumberland; and this proportion appears to have been substantially maintained until after the Revolution. In 1782, of ninety thousand pounds State tax, Salem was required to raise three thousand and fifty-seven pounds, and Cumberland about one-third less, namely, two thousand and twenty-five pounds. This last proportion still continues. The State tax of 1868 was 350,000 dollars, of which Salem raised 12,880 dollars, and Cumberland 8079 dollars.

It appears from the census of the two counties taken at different periods, that Cumberland has gained on Salem in population, but not in wealth.

Census of Salem and Cumberland.

	1790	1800	1810	1820	1830
Salem	10,437	11,371	12,761	14,022	14,155
Cumberland . . .	8,248	9,529	12,670	12,668	14,093

	1840	1850	1860	1865	1869 estimated
Salem	16,024	19,467	22,458	23,162	24,000
Cumberland . . .	14,374	17,189	22,605	26,233	33,000

4

CHAPTER III.

In 1754, Daniel Elmer, who was a surveyor, and the oldest son of Rev. Daniel Elmer, pastor of the Fairfield Presbyterian Church, laid out for Alexander Moore a town on the east side of the Cohansey, which it was proposed to call Cumberland. The streets were laid out at right angles, and the squares contained each $18\frac{1}{2}$ square perches. It extended from what is now Jefferson Street to a little north of the present iron works on the north, and from the river to about as far east as where Orange Street now is. Some of the old title-deeds refer to this plan, but the streets were never opened. Most of the site was then the original forest.

The road to Deerfield was laid out in 1768, upon the old travelled track from the bridge to near the corner of the present Commerce and Pearl Streets, thence northerly, a little south of where Pearl Street now is. In 1785, the road to Fairfield was changed, and laid out to begin at John Westcott's stone house—then a low one-story stone house—standing at the southeast corner of the present Commerce and Pearl Streets, afterwards for years owned and occupied by Mark Riley, the lot extending up to where Orange Street now is; thence southward along the present Pearl Street, over the dam made by Col. Enos Seeley, and thence along what is now the left hand road to the brick-kiln corner, and thence south along the old road over Rocap's Run.

John Moore White having been licensed to practise law, and married, came to Bridgeton in 1791 and erected a handsome dwelling, now forming a part of the hotel at the corner of Commerce and Laurel Streets. He procured the road to be changed and to run as it does now, called Laurel Street. He laid out himself and fenced some of the other streets to correspond. His lot, inclosed with a handsome fence, and well improved with shade and fruit trees, and an extensive, well laid-out garden, extended on Commerce Street from the corner of Laurel to the present Water Street, and on Laurel Street from the corner to James Hood's line.

The present livery stables were his barn and stables, the tide in the river flowing up to near the building. North of him it was an open woods, in which the laurel was so conspicuous as to give the name Laurel Hill to the elevated ground still called by that name. The present Pearl Street was by him called Middle Street. Bank was called Freemason Street, and Washington was called Point Street. The road to Deerfield, after passing the first run north of the town, was very crooked. It was made straight in 1796 about half way, and a few years later as the turnpike now runs. The turnpike was made in 1852. The straight road to Fairton was opened in 1799 ; that to Millville in 1805. In 1810, the road to Buckshootem was laid. The turnpike was made to Millville in 1853.

The road from Greenwich to Bridgeton, through Bowentown, was in use by the early settlers. In 1769, it was regularly laid out as a four-rod road, and then passed the court-house, down the hill to Water Street (now Atlantic), thence a straight course to the foot of the bridge. The road, however, was a deep gully below the court-house until about 1802, when George Burgin, a prominent citizen, who had built the stone storehouse at the corner of Broad and Atlantic Streets, made the road passable for carriages, and caused the wharf it leads to to be erected. In 1800, the present Atlantic Street was laid as it now is ; but for several years the old road passing in front of the Parvin House continued to be used by carriages, and was the foot-path until that house was taken away in 1825. The road from the foot of the bridge up the hill, and thence along what is now Franklin Street, was laid nearly as it now is in 1771. For many years, however, this road up the hill was a mere sandy track, but little used. In 1825, the late Dr. Ephraim Buck, having had the office of overseer imposed on him, put it in good order, at an expense much complained of by the tax-payers, but which soon made it the main thoroughfare of travel, and proved an excellent improvement. The old middle road down the hill, which was never regularly laid out, was shut up in 1815. The straight road to Roadstown was, after several futile attempts, laid out and opened about 1798. Broad Street was formerly called Main Street. Until after the Revolution, Bridgeton was but an insignificant hamlet, having not more than from 150 to 200 inhabitants. The houses built up to that time were in the neighborhood of the court-house, and on Vine and Main Streets, and on Commerce and Laurel Streets, south

of Commerce. The bridge had no draw, and was a subject of considerable contention. The Rev. Philip Fithian, then a tutor in Virginia, visited the place in 1774. He records in his journal under the
date of April 26, "visited Nathan Leak (in Deerfield). He told me
the beginning and continuation of the quarrel of the magistrates, freeholders, and other officers, about raising money for repairing Cohan-
seyBridge." This quarrel grew out of a dispute about its location ;
a strong party, headed by Col. Enos Seeley, owner of the property
on the creek below Jefferson Street, being in favor of putting it
opposite Broad Street, while Alexander Moore and his friends insisted upon retaining the old site. Nothing but indispensable
repairs was done to the old bridge until after Mr. White took possession of his property. He was desirous of having a draw, so that
he might erect wharves above; and to induce the freeholders to
incur the necessary expense, agreed to defray the cost of the draw,
and keep it in good repair five years; and he also deeded to trustees a lot of land on the river, where the rolling and pipe-mills
now are, to be used as a free public landing for wood and lumber.
The lot was so used for many years, but becoming less and less
important to the community, Mr. White—on the ground that the
conditions of his grant had not been complied with—some twenty-
five years ago took possession of it and sold it. The town is certainly far more benefited by its present use than it could be if held
for its original purpose. From 1799 to 1801, the present stone
abutments were put up, and the bridge was built on piles, and
raised much higher than it had been, and at this time the dispute
about its location was renewed, George Burgin being desirous of
having it placed opposite Broad Street.* Old inhabitants speak of
the tide having risen above the floor in former times. The draw
has been several times altered. For many years it was raised up;
but it was a constant source of trouble and expense. There not
having been any previous law authorizing this bridge, one was
passed in 1834. The existing structure was built in 1849. The
street on both sides of the bridge has been raised from five to eight
feet.

An actual enumeration of the inhabitants made in 1792, found
that they numbered 300. About this time General Giles built the

* Now, in 1869, arrangements have been made for building a bridge at Broad
Street, so that soon, instead of only one, there will be three.

house on Broad Street, now occupied by Rev. Dr. Jones, and shortly after this, several pretty good houses were erected. That occupied by Mrs. Read was built by Ebenezer Miller; but it has been enlarged and much improved. All the houses occupied in 1748 have long ago disappeared. Among the early business men of the town was Col. David Potter. His wharf and store-house were on the west side of the river, next below the Mason line. His dwelling—a wooden structure at the northwest corner of Broad and Franklin Streets—was burned about the year 1780, and he then built the present brick dwelling and store at the same place. In his day, a considerable quantity of wheat, raised in Hopewell, Deerfield, and Pittsgrove, was brought to this place and exported to Philadelphia, and the Brandywine Mills. He died in 1805. Next after him were Seeley and Merseilles, who had a store near the southeast corner of the bridge. Merseilles built the store-house at the southeast corner of Commerce and Laurel Streets. He also built a good dwelling-house opposite, now a part of Grosscup's building. The town being at the head of navigation, a considerable business in carrying wood and lumber to Philadelphia grew up; but up to the beginning of the present century not more than three or four vessels were owned in the place, nor did the stores fairly compete with those at Greenwich. In 1780, a letter-of-marque schooner, called Gov. Livingston, was built on the Cohansey, at the place now occupied as a lumber yard by Messrs. Mulford, which made one successful trip. Upon her return from her second voyage, with a valuable cargo, she was captured near the Delaware by a British frigate.

The sons of Col. Potter first kept the store at the southwest corner of Commerce and Laurel Streets. The most influential citizens in 1800 were Dr. Jonathan Elmer, Col. Potter, Ebenezer Seeley, Jonathan Bowen, Dr. Samuel M. Shute, James Burch, Zachariah Lawrence, Enoch Boon, John Moore White, and Gen. Giles. Ebenezer Elmer, who had been previously in practice as a physician, and was a prominent public man, moved on to a farm at Bowtown in 1795, from whence he returned in 1807. Col. Enos Seeley had become disabled by disease, and Judge Ephraim Seeley, son of Col. Ephraim, died in 1799, soon after finishing his house at the corner of Commerce and Bank Streets.

We have no means of knowing what was the precise number of inhabitants at this epoch, but they may be estimated to have been about four hundred. Nearly every house then existing can be identified. On the east side was the old Seeley mansion at the mill, now gone; a house on Commerce Street nearly opposite the Methodist meeting-house, built by Mr. Fauver, on a lot at the southeast corner of John Moore White's property; the house at the corner of Commerce and Bank Streets, built by Ephraim Seeley; the academy on Bank Street, having, as now, the Masonic lodge in the upper story, and the house on the north side of Irving, fronting Bank, then owned by Ebenezer Seeley; a house on the south side of Irving, west of Bank Street; the old stone house at the southeast corner of Commerce and Pearl Streets, long owned by Mark Riley; five houses on Pearl, south of Commerce; house near the saw-mill, then owned by Col. Enos Seeley, long known as the house of Widow Jay; the house of his son, David Seeley, now Mrs. Buck's, fronting on Laurel; the old Boyd mansion opposite; five houses on the east side of Laurel, south of Commerce; one stone house on the west side; store-houses at the south corners of Commerce and Laurel Streets; a house and a shoemaker-shop a little west of it, built by James Burch, on the south side of Commerce Street (now James Potter's); a store-house near the southeast corner of the bridge; the old mansion of Alexander Moore, then a tavern, and two houses near thereto; White's mansion house, now the hotel; the house of Eden M. Merseilles, now a part of Grosscup's building; a house east of this built by Reuben Burgin; a blacksmith-shop at the corner of Commerce and Pearl; a house on the east side of Pearl Street, now S. W. Seeley's; a house where the brick Presbyterian church stands; one nearly opposite owned by James Hood, a Scotchman, then following his business of making wrought nails, and his shop; a blacksmith-shop on Washington Street near the corner of Laurel; the stone house on the side of Laurel, nearly opposite Irving Street; two small houses near thereto; three houses above on the same street, and a store-house at the northeast corner of Laurel and Irving.

On the west side were the old Parvin House near the foot of the bridge and a stone house north of it, on Commerce Street, the old Cotting House, then Enoch Boon's; four other houses on Atlantic Street; a house on Broad Street below the jail; three houses on the north side of Broad near the court-house, one of which was then occupied as a tavern; two houses on the west side of Franklin Street; Col. Potter's house and store at the corner of Broad and Franklin; two or three houses between that and Giles Street; the mansion of Gen. Giles; two or three houses above on the same side; six or seven houses on the south side of Broad Street; three houses on the west side of Fayette Street; a large three-storied house where the court-house now stands, long occupied as a tavern, and five or six houses on Vine Street; a one-story school house where the public school now is, and the old brick Presbyterian church. The court-house stood in the middle of Broad Street. The only wharves at this time were a small one just below the bridge on the west side, another of better construction lower down on the same side, belonging to Col. Potter, and one on the east side constructed by Seeley & Merseilles, about twenty rods below the bridge, with the remains of the old Smith Wharf on the property now Mrs. Buck's. The wharves above the bridge were not built until after the draw was made, so that masted vessels could pass through. Among the first were those of Laurel Hill, now disused. Goose Hill above got its name from the circumstance that the owner of the farm opposite accused Abraham Sayre, who lived at the northern end of the town, of plucking the feathers from some of his geese, and shortly afterwards some of his pigs happening to go astray, he set up advertisements offering a reward for them, and hoping that Squire Sayre had not mistaken them for geese and pulled off the hair. This brought on a suit for libel, about 1810. The suit was settled by an arbitration; but the name Goose Hill became the popular usage.

About the year 1800, Levi Leake, of Deerfield, brother of the eminent lawyer Samuel Leake, and a warm Federalist, commenced building a new house on a lot he owned near where the pipe-mill stands. Before it was finished, Mr. Jefferson was elected President, which so displeased him that he made a vow that he would not complete the building until the Federalists came again into power. As this never happened, the building remained near twenty years unoccupied, until on his death it was sold and removed, standing now on the north side of Laurel Street, near to the corner of Washington.

The following houses have at different times been occupied as taverns: A house on the west side of Laurel Street above Irving, which was burnt in 1826; the hotel, the old Moore mansion, the old Parvin House, the double stone house on the west side of Atlantic Street, the house opposite the jail, the Cohansey Hotel, a large house standing on the present site of the court-house, the

house of Dr. Hampton, on Vine Street, and the house at the southwest corner of Broad and Giles Streets.

The number of families in 1829 was found to be 342, and the
population 1736. Just previous to this the east side of the river
began to outnumber the other side. There were then four taverns
and ten stores. Twenty-five vessels belonging to the place were
employed principally in the wood trade, besides several oyster
boats. Upwards of 25,000 cords of wood were sent annually to
Philadelphia.

In 1838, the number of inhabitants was found to be 2315, of
whom 1513 were on the east side and 802 on the west. The
growth during the preceding ten years had been almost exclusively
on the east side. There were still four taverns and about twelve
stores. At this time the streets were named as they are now
known. The streets since opened are Orange, Pine, Walnut,
Church, Cedar, and Elmer Streets on the east side, and Academy,
Oak, and Hampton Streets on the west side. In 1850 the population of the town was 3303. In 1860 it had increased to fully 5000,
which may be considered as the present population.—Two taverns
are now found sufficient instead of the four maintained when there
were not half so many inhabitants.

The journal of a young lady who visited Bridgeton in 1786,
before mentioned, gives the name of the place Cohansey, and it is
to be regretted that this old Indian name was not adopted as the
name of this town, instead of being only the name of one of the
townships (and since dropped entirely), containing hardly one
third of the inhabitants. She mentions leaving Cooper's ferry
(Camden) about 12 o'clock, part of the company in Mr. Potter's
family wagon, Mr. Moore and I in his carriage, the latter being the
old-fashioned one horse chaise, then lately introduced. They
travelled through Gloucester, Woodbury, Greenwich, now Clarksboro, to the Pine Tavern, where they passed the night. This was
a well-known wayside inn, now disused, about four miles beyond
the Pole Tavern, which was also a noted house of entertainment
before the Revolution. It was cold, and she complained of the
scanty clothing on the beds, and that the windows were not glazed,
and had no shutters, only boards nailed up, and these an inch
apart. They left at 6 A. M. and called at Dr. Harris', in Pittsgrove, who married a daughter of Alexander Moore, some of whose
descendants are still living. She records frequent visits to Moore

Hall. On Sunday went to church at New England Town. The next Sunday Mr. Grier preached in the court-house; visited Mrs. Boyd, mother of the then wife of Colonel Potter, where she was staying. "We strolled about in her garden; it is situated along the creek, and is really beautiful. Well might a poet sit under the rural willows and contemplate the beauties of nature and art. There were many beautiful flowers. Three sloops came up whilst we stood there, and cast anchor." This dwelling and garden have long since disappeared. It was one of the old time mansions, which the writer remembers to have seen more than fifty years ago dilapidated and empty. It was just above where the new bridge from Broad Street is to cross. Mrs. Boyd was one of those excellent Christian women whose memory deserves to be perpetuated. Her husband, from the north of Ireland, came over to this country about the year 1772, leaving his wife and three children in their native home. After following the occupation of a peddler for a short time, he succeeded in commencing a store at Cohansey Bridge, and then sent for his wife and children. They left Ireland in the fall of 1773, but on their arrival, found that Mr. Boyd had recently died. The widow took upon herself the charge of her husband's store, and aided by an excellent clerk, James Ewing, the father of the late Chief Justice Ewing, whose mother was her eldest daughter, she succeeded in maintaining her family in comfort. Her only son, at the time of his father's death about six years old, was a promising young man, but having entered into business in Philadelphia, died of the yellow fever in 1795. The youngest daughter became the second wife of Colonel Potter, with whom her mother resided for some years before her death, ending her days in 1812 at the good old age of 80 years. The margin of the creek, on the east side, with the exception of the wharf near the bridge, and that of Seeley & Merseilles' lower down, was a low meadow until within the last twenty years.

Before the Revolution very few covered carriages were in use. Travelling by men was almost exclusively on horseback, the women riding on side-saddles, and frequently behind their male friends on pillions. Sleighs and sleds were used in winter, before carriages were common. Philip Fithian, whose journal has been referred to, travelled to Virginia on horseback in 1773, crossing the ferry from Elsinborough to Port Penn, Delaware, which was then much in use, but has been long discontinued. Dr. Jonathan Elmer travelled the same route to take his seat in Congress at Baltimore, in November, 1776, returning in February by way of Philadelphia, not being then able to cross the river lower down in consequence of the ice. A memorandum of his expenses still remains, from which the following items are extracted :—

1776.

Dec. 27, Paid J. Housman,	12s.	6d.	Dec. 29, at Rogers',	6s.	0d.
at Port Penn,	3	3	at Bushtown,	2	6
at Aiken's,	3	0	at Buck's,		9
" 28, at Boid's,	6	6	at Rush's, (Balt.),	1	9
at Charlestown,	6	6			
at Stevenson's,	1	9			

1777.

Feb. 15, for keeping horse in the country five weeks,	£1	17s.	6d.	Dec. 18 at Marcus Hook,	3s.	9d.
				" 20, at Indian Queen, (Phila.)	10	0
" 17, Rodger's ferry,		12	6	at Sally Westcott's,	2	6
at Stevenson's,		1	6	at Cooper's ferry,	3	0
at Bird's,		3	2	at Haddonfield,	3	6
at Christeen,		5	0	at Eldridge's,	4	5
" 18, at Newport,		6	3	at Pine Tavern,	2	6
at Wilmington,		4	3			

The Charlestown above mentioned was in Cecil County, Maryland; Rodger's ferry was over the Susquehanna; Eldridge's is believed to be the old death of the Fox Tavern in Gloucester County, near where Clarksboro' now is. The currency was the proclamation money at seven and sixpence the dollar.

Another memorandum details the expenses of a horseback journey from Bridgeton to Morristown, the head-quarters of the American army, which he visited as one of the committee of Congress on Hospitals. It commenced March 12, 1777, the first item being at Champney's 2s. This was at the Pole Tavern, then kept by the Widow Champney, mother of Dr. Champney; then comes Pine Tavern and Eldridge's; 13th was spent in Philadelphia; 14th and 15th visit to Haddonfield, where some of our troops then were; 16th to Burlington; 17th at Rocky Hill (near Princeton), 18th at Col. Potter's quarters (he then had the command of a regiment of militia); 20th and 21st at Baskenridge and Morristown, 22d to Trenton, and then to Philadelphia, which he left on the 31st, and home by Eldridge's, Pine Tavern, and Widow Champney's. The total expense of the trip was £7 10s., or nearly $20. In April it is noted, paid Tybout for a hat (no doubt a beaver)

£3 5s., or $8.66. Such a hat of good quality lasted on careful heads five or six, and even ten years.

The land titles in Bridgeton are held under four different surveys. A tract called the eleven thousand acre survey was located for the West Jersey Society in 1686, but was not then recorded. In 1716 this tract was resurveyed. It begins at a pine tree on the northeast side of the Cohansey, about two miles below the bridge; runs from thence east about two miles; then north, then west to the Cohansey, some two miles above the bridge, and then down the river to the beginning. Jeremiah Basse was for some time the agent of this Society, and seems to have had, or claimed to have, some right to the property; but the right of his heirs and devisees was released to Alexander Moore, including the old Hancock mill and adjoining property.

One of the London proprietors of West Jersey was named John Bridges. The Rev. Thomas Bridges graduated at Harvard in 1675, then went to England, and returned in 1682 with testimonials from Owen and other eminent dissenting ministers. He was for a time a merchant, but after he became a preacher went to the West Indies. He was probably a son or near relative of John Bridges. He came to Cohansey, and preached in the old Fairfield church. In 1697 Thomas Revel made a deed to him reciting, "Whereas the Honorable West Jersey Society in England have, upon the consideration mentioned in their letter to Thomas Bridges, dated July 19, 1692, therein and thereby given, or proposed to give, to the said Thomas Bridges, in fee forever, 1000 acres of land of and belonging to the said Society within the said province of West Jersey, in what situation he should please to take up the same," and that said Revel being seized of 4000 acres by virtue of a deed from Jeremiah Basse, agent of said Society, he therefore conveys to him 1000 acres. By virtue of this deed a survey was at the same date made by Joshua Barkstead for Bridges, beginning at a pine tree standing on the north side of Mill Creek, about half way between the saw-mill and then going over across the run to the Indian Fields (which was a little above the present road to Milville); thence north 336 perches to a corner tree. The side lines run east and west, and the tract was surveyed for 1050 acres, of which 50 acres were for one Collett, to be held in common with Bridges, and he to have a proportional share of the Indian Fields. This tract was afterwards known as the Indian

Fields tract, and was the first settled in the neighborhood, the titles being held under Bridges. The beginning corner was back of the Commerce Street Methodist meeting-house, the only part of the north line now marked being the fence between the graveyard and the parsonage lot, and it runs thence so as to strike the house fronting Bank Street, west of the railroad, and thence (it is supposed) to the tree so well known as the umbrella or sunset tree. Col. Ephraim Seeley for many years owned the land east of this line, up to Irving Street; he devised it to his son Ephraim, from whom it descended to his children. Upon the division of the latter property in 1800, this line, which in 1697 was run due north, was run N. 4¾ W.; and in 1848 it was run N. 2½ W., thus showing the variation of the compass, as practically used, between those dates. Bridges had also a survey made for him on the Cohansey, bounding on Fuller Creek, since called Rocap's Run. This survey calls also for the line of the township of Pamphylia. Such a township was never formed, but it is probable there was a fulling-mill on the run, such a mill being almost as indispensable for the new settlement as a saw-mill.

Bridges' Indian Field tract appears to have been subdivided for him into tracts of fifty acres, which he sold out as purchasers and settlers offered. One William Dare, described as of Cohansey, in the county of Salem, who probably came into this region with the Fairfield people, had located a tract of 100 acres of cedar swamp on Lebanon, as early as March, 1695–6. About 1700 he became the owner of two fifty-acre tracts, as set off by Bridges, comprising a part of the farm northeast of Elmer's mill-pond, recently occupied by David Dare, one of his lineal descendants, who died April, 1863. About 1753 William Dare, son of the William first above named, and Col. Ephraim Seeley, purchased of the agent of the West Jersey Society several hundred acres lying south of Bridge's tract, and east of the tract sold to Moore. Most of the Indian Field settlers, who were the first in the eastern part of Bridgeton, were from Fairfield. Among them, besides Dare, were Riley and Loomis— or Lummis, as the name has been since written—and Hood. Hobert Hood's tract was a part of the Society land, purchased by him at an early date.

In 1752 Alexander Moore, of Cohansey Bridge, purchased of the agents of the West Jersey Society 990 acres, part of their 11,000 acre tract. This purchase begins on the Cohansey, a little above Pamphylia Spring, and runs several courses to Bridges' Indian Fields tract, striking it a little east of the beginning corner, thence along said tract, and several courses north of it to the Cohansey, something more than a mile above the town. By means of this deed, and of a release from one Pigeon, a claimant under Basse, of the tract connected with the Hancock mill, he became the owner of all that part of East Bridgeton lying west of Bridges' line. That line was probably so run in consequence of the mill tract being held by Hancock. Moore was of Irish descent, and was the first person who transacted much business at Cohansey Bridge. His grandson, the late Judge John Moore White, thought he came here about 1730, and married into the Reeve family. He accumulated a very handsome estate, built himself a good house near his store, on the north side of Commerce Street, near the corner of Water, in which a tavern was kept for many years after his death, and which was removed to make room for the present brick building about 1830. He died at a good old age in 1786, on the farm now attached to the poor-house, where he, and his son after him, had an establishment known as Moore Hall. At his death there was a protracted lawsuit about the probate of his will. It appears by the depositions on file, that he had been paid by several of his debtors in depreciated continental money, when it was a legal tender, and he used to carry about him, and very frequently show to others, what he called his rogues' list of these debtors. The will, however, was confirmed. He devised his Bridgeton and much other property to his three grandsons, the three children of his daughter, a beautiful woman, who married an Englishman, a merchant in Philadelphia, named John White, who, during the Revolutionary War, was aid to Gen. Sullivan, and was killed in the attack on Chew's house in Germantown. Mrs. White died in 1770, leaving an infant, and lies buried with her father and mother in the graveyard at Greenwich. John Moore White, her youngest child, became of age in 1791, just previous to which time the land, except that in Bridgeton, was divided between the three brothers, by order of the Orphans' Court. In the course of a few years the two elder brothers, Alexander and William, died without issue, so that the Bridgeton property became vested in John. All of the tract within the limits of the town, lying south of Commerce Street, appears to have been sold by Alexander Moore in his lifetime, or released to persons who claimed it; but all the land north of that street became the property of John Moore White, who commenced selling lots in 1792, and in 1810 conveyed all the unsold residue to William Potter and Jeremiah Buck.

The titles west of the Cohansey, are held under three different surveys. The first was made for Robert Hutchinson, May 27th, 1786, for 950 acres. The north line of this tract cornered at a white oak on the Cohansey, marked H, standing in the hollow near the river, above the place of going over to Richard Hancock's mill. Above this was a survey made for Cornelius Mason, in 1689, for 5000 acres. As originally described it began at the bound tree of Robert Hutchinson, standing in a valley by the west-northwest side of the north branch of the river Cohanzick, thence up the river, to a white oak tree standing upon a hill near the branch in an Indian old field, thence W. N. W. 800 perches. Mason, who was a London trader, called this tract "Winchcomb manor," after a manor of that name he owned in England. The original survey was taken to England and never recorded until 1764. The farm lying above Muddy Branch, as the stream, now a pond, just above the iron works was formerly called, appears to have been partially cleared by the Indians, who had a burial place on it, since called Coffin Point. As early as 1697 one John Garrison settled and built a house on it, and about 1715 built a house of cedar logs, near the bridge, in which Benjamin Seeley lived. About 1734 Silas Parvin purchased the land of Garrison south of Muddy Branch, and in 1741 that lying north of the branch. But Parvin's right to the property was disputed by Mason, and about 1741 suits were commenced which were in some way compromised. After this the persons claiming to be Mason's heirs conveyed the whole tract to Israel Pemberton, a friend, residing in Philadelphia, and he commenced suits. In the progress of the controversy the land was resurveyed, and a jury of view settled the corner to be twenty perches south of the bridge, where it has been ever since held to be. The south line runs thence through at the middle of Oak Street, and a little south of the academy. It was supposed for a time that the Hutchinson survey cornered at the same place, and Cotting took a conveyance for a considerable tract under that title in 1739. It was, however, ascertained that the true corner of the Hutchinson survey was at the place formerly called the shipyard, now the lumber yard of Messrs. Mulford. This left a considerable tract of land between the two surveys unclaimed, which Ebenezer Miller, a deputy surveyor, residing in Greenwich, and a Friend, in 1749 covered with a survey containing 427 acres, under whom the titles of the land, from Oak Street on the north to a considerable distance south of Vine Street are held.

Silas Parvin laid a survey of 20 acres on the land where his house stood; and dying in 1779, his son Clarence remained in possession of the house, and set up a claim to all the land between Muddy Branch and the Mason line, a part of which he transferred to Dr. Jonathan Elmer. During the war of the Revolution, Pemberton, being ranked as a Tory, took no steps to vindicate his title; but in 1783 he commenced an ejectment against Parvin, which does not appear to have been tried. In 1788 Parvin died insolvent, and shortly afterwards Parvin died; and his heir proving insolvent, his property was sold by the sheriff, and purchased by Jonathan Bowen, who released to Dr. Elmer the part lying west of Franklin Street, and these persons, or those claiming under them, have ever since been in possession of the property, now of great value. It is probable that the Parvin title was also sold by the sheriff, but no deed is on record, or now known to exist. Jonathan Bowen conveyed a part of the property, including the old Parvin house, to his son Smith in 1790, and, dying in 1804, devised the remainder retained by him, including the sites of the iron works and grist-mill, to his said son and to his grandchildren.

It is probable that Ebenezer Miller laid out Broad Street its present width of 100 feet, like the Main street of Greenwich, but there is no record of either. No law having for a long time existed authorizing streets so wide, the overseers declined to keep them in order, and hence a section was inserted in the general road act, declaring these two streets to be lawful highways. Commerce Street, above Franklin, was not opened until about 1805, when Dr. Elmer opened it. Since, it has been regularly laid out. An old plan, which was never carried out, proposed to lay out that part of the town west of the river into regular squares.

The first notice of a stage to Philadelphia that has been discovered, occurs in the journal of Mr. Fithian, April 22, 1774; he records: "Rode to the stage early for the papers." His father, at whose house he was then on a visit, lived in Greenwich, near to Sheppard's mill. It is supposed the stage stopped at Roadstown. May 2, he records: "Very early I rode over to Mr. Hollinshead's (he was the minister at New England Town, and then lived on the parsonage in Sayre's Neck) at Miss Pratt's request, to carry her to Mr. Hoshel's, to be ready to-morrow morning for the stage. Dined at Mrs. Boyd's (Bridgeton), and after dinner we rode to Mr. Hoshel's. 3d, I conducted Miss Pratt to the stage this morning by 5 o'clock."

A letter from Martha Boyd, afterwards Mrs. Ewing, to her mother, dated Allentown, March 16, 1778, says: "We left Mr. Hoshel's at 12 o'clock night; we had eight passengers, middling clever, and arrived at Cooper's ferry at 3 o'clock in the afternoon. The next morning at nine o'clock, set sail in the stage boat for Bordentown where we arrived at noon."

Mr. Hoshel lived in Upper Hopewell, not far from the Salem County line, and probably kept a tavern, and was the proprietor of the stage. During or not long after the Revolution, this or some other stage line was started from Bridgeton, making two trips a week, at first by the way of Roadstown, but afterwards one trip on that route, and one by the way of Deerfield; and so it continued to go until about the year 1806, when it went up one day and down the next. In 1809, when Mr. White's house was changed to a hotel, a stage was started from there to run up and down on the alternate days, and to go through in a shorter time.—The two lines were afterwards consolidated, and there has always since been, until the opening of the railway, a daily stage both ways between this place and Philadelphia. For many years the time for starting was at sunrise.

Until after the establishment of the federal government, all the correspondence in this part of the State had to depend upon private conveyances. There was indeed before this time no post-route in New Jersey, except the main road between Philadelphia and New York. In 1792, while Jonathan Elmer was senator, a post-route was established from Philadelphia to Salem, and thence to Bridge-town. Between the latter places the mail was carried once a week, on horseback or in a sulky, for ten years, the post-office being kept by John Soulard, at his house on Broad, near the corner of Fayette Street. In 1802, after Ebenezer Elmer became a member of Congress, a mail-route was established from Woodbury to Bridgeton, Millville, Port Elizabeth and Cape May. The first carriers, beginning in 1804, were Benaiah Parvin and son, who kept a tavern in the old mansion house of Alexander Moore. James Burch, who built and owned the house opposite, now James

B. Potter's, was the postmaster; and it is remembered that the letters were kept in the front parlor and handed from the window, then so high above the walk as to be barely reached by the raised hand. The mail was carried on Monday by way of Roadstown, and returned on Wednesday by the same route. On Thursday it was carried by way of Deerfield, returning on Saturday the same way. A daily mail commenced about 1816. The postmaster who succeeded James Burch was Abijah Harris, who lived nearly opposite. After him, Stephen Lupton kept the office in his shoemaker shop, on the north side of Washington Street, about half way between Laurel and Pearl. About 1818 he resigned, and was succeeded by Curtis Ogden, who held the office longer than any other incumbent, keeping it in his tailor shop, south side of Commerce Street, about where Brewster's store now is. Jeremiah Lupton superseded him in 1842, then Daniel B. Thompson from 1845 to 1850, then S. P. Kirkbride until 1854, then Henry Sheppard until 1861, when Geo. W. Johnson, the present incumbent, was appointed.

A steamboat company was incorporated in 1845, and a fine steamboat, called the Cohansey, ran regularly to Philadelphia; but the length of the water route, about 80 miles, made it difficult for a day boat to compete with the route by way of Salem, partly by stage and partly by boat, and with the regular daily stages, and it was soon found that the enterprise must be abandoned. The boat was therefore sold, and after running a year or two by private parties, was withdrawn. A night boat, which ran for two or three years recently, was more successful.

The West Jersey Railroad Company was incorporated in 1853, and contemplated a road from Camden to Cape May; but owing to financial and other difficulties, it was at first completed and put in operation only to Woodbury. But in 1859 the road from Glassboro' to Millville was made, and the impetus thus given to the original West Jersey Company, brought about the completion of their road from Woodbury to Bridgeton, which was opened in July, 1861. The terminus of this road, it is supposed, will always remain at Bridgeton, and the original design of connecting Philadelphia with Cape May will be carried out by extending the road to the latter place from Millville, now nearly complete.

A gas company was incorporated, and succeeded in completing the present works in November, 1858. Soon after this, the township committees of the townships of Bridgeton and Cohansey were

5

constituted a joint board, with power to raise money by tax for lighting the streets, which is now done, and also with power to grade and regulate the streets. A grade has accordingly been adopted, in accordance with which Commerce Street, west of the bridge, and other streets in Cohansey were graded in 1861, at an expense which has been much complained of, as was the first attempt at this kind of improvement, made by Dr. Buck, a quarter of a century sooner.

In the year 1814 Messrs. James Lee, then of Port Elizabeth, and Ebenezer Seeley, of Bridgeton, who had purchased from Abraham Sayre, Esq., the land lying on the east side of the main stream of the Cohansey, joined with Smith Bowen, who owned the property on the west side of the stream, in erecting the dam, thus forming the water power still in use. Bowen sold his half of the water power to Benjamin Reeves and David Reeves of Camden, who commenced the erection of the iron works the same year, and commenced making nails in 1815. They were cut for many years of the best Swedish iron, across the grain of the metal. The writer remembers to have seen, in the year 1805, the first machine for cutting and heading nails at one operation ever invented. It was on Crosswicks Creek, in Burlington County, and was comparatively very complicated. The patent having been obtained by the Messrs. Reeves, was soon very much simplified.

At first the nails sold for from 10 to 15 cents per pound, now they sell for $3\frac{1}{2}$ cents. Very soon the Cumberland nails obtained a preference in the market, which has never been lost. In 1824 a fire having consumed the building first erected, the works were rebuilt and enlarged and the whole establishment greatly improved. Seeley and Lee not having the capital to use their half of the water power to advantage, were obliged to reconvey it to Mr. Sayre. He erected a flour mill on the east side opposite Coffin Point, which was used as a grist-mill for a few years, but on his death in 1820 the mill and water power were purchased by Messrs. Reeves, who then became the owners of the whole water power. The grist-mill was taken down and removed to the works on the west side, where after a few years it was burned up.

The rolling-mill operated by steam on the east side of the creek was erected in 1847 and in 1853 the building used for manufacturing gas pipe was put up. About the year 1843 a great change was made in the mode of cutting the nails, by means of which a much superior nail can be made from inferior iron. The iron is rolled in sheets 12 or 15 inches wide, which are then slit into strips of a width, corresponding with the length of the nail to be produced. Then the nails are cut lengthwise of the grain of the metal instead of crosswise as before. This establishment has always been well conducted and has been one of the principal means of advancing the growth and prosperity of the town. When in full operation about 400 hands are employed, mostly heads of families, who have been profitably employed, and have contributed in their turn to the business of other mechanics and traders. There are twenty furnaces, two trains of rolls and 102 nail machines, the annual product, in favorable years, being 100,000 kegs of nails and 1,500,000 feet of gas pipe.

Benjamin Reeves, one of the original founders, died in 1844. Other partners have been from time to time admitted. In 1856 the concern became an incorporated company, by the name of the Cumberland Nail and Iron Works, and is under the management of Robert C. Nichols, Esq. The value of its real estate, as assessed, is 266,000 dollars; the capital of the company being 350,000 dollars.

About the year 1818 Benjamin Reeves conveyed to the late Daniel P. Stratton the undivided half part of a lot of land, where the grist-mill stands, and half a sufficient quantity of water to drive a first class merchant flour-mill, it being the intention that Mr. Stratton and Mr. David Reeves should erect the mill together as joint owners. But doubts soon arose whether water power for such a purpose could be safely spared, without endangering the iron works, and Mr. Reeves declined to build the mill. Mr. Stratton then applied for a division of the lot, and one half being set off to him, he proceeded to erect the existing flour mill in 1822. The quantity of water he had a right to use was adjusted by an arbitration.

As the business of the iron works was from time to time increased, and as the quantity of water furnished by the seven distinct streams entering into and forming Cohansey River, diminished, it was found that the water power sometimes failed. To remedy this it was at first proposed to increase the power by putting a dam across the river where the bridge now is that connects the works; and for this purpose an act of the legislature was obtained in 1839. But before this purpose was carried into effect, the plan was devised of heating the boilers necessary to drive a powerful steam engine, by means of the same fires that heat the iron, which fully succeeded, so that the dam was never erected, and after a time the rolling of iron at the works on the west side, which required so great a supply of water, was abandoned.

About the year 1825 those persons in the town who kept a horse were so much annoyed by applications to lend or hire him, that a livery stable was started by a joint stock company, and so carried on five or six years, until like most concerns of the kind it was found unprofitable and the stock was sold at a loss of more than half the original capital. This start, however, effected the object, one or more livery stables, kept by different individuals, have been continued ever since. For several years past the business has been rather overdone, there being now four.

The glass works were established in 1836 by the firm of Stratton, Buck & Co. After the death of Mr. Buck, in 1841, the business was carried on by a joint stock company which did not succeed. For a time window glass was made. After passing through several hands it was enlarged, in 1855, and is now in successful operation, the yearly product being about $130,000.

It may be remarked that for about twenty years the firm of Stratton & Buck carried on the largest business that was done in the county. This firm and that of Bowie and Shannon from 1812 to 1836 in the stone store at the corner of Broad and Atlantic Streets, transacted a heavy retail business, and brought to the place customers from all the surrounding districts.

It is doubtful whether any newspapers were regularly received in Bridgeton until after 1775. In that year an association was formed, of which Ebenezer Elmer, then a student of medicine, was the Secretary, by the members of which weekly papers on various topics were written, and these being copied, were left at the tavern kept by Matthew Potter (believed to have been the house next east of the present Cohansey Hotel), to be there perused by such as chose. Among the writers of those papers were Dr. Jonathan Elmer, Joseph Bloomfield, Dr. Lewis Howell, and his brother Richard, afterwards Governor of the State.

Previous to this time, about 1773, a society existed, which generally met in Bridgeton, but of which several young persons residing in Greenwich, Fithians and Ewings, who were then distinguished for intelligence, and for the beauty of some of the females, were members, called the Admonishing Society. Communications were made to this society in writing, anonymously, admonishing members of faults, and on other subjects, which were read at the meetings. If the members admonished thought it necessary, they were allowed to defend themselves, or replies might be made in writing. Of this society, Robert Patterson, from Ireland, who then kept a store in Bridgeton, was a member. By way of enlivening the proceedings, he sent in written proposals for a wife, giving the requisite qualifications, which left one young lady, from whom, in her old age, this detail was received, who it was said had refused him, too young. Another lady, however, sportively answered the challenge, and what was thus begun in sport ended in marriage, and a long and happy union. The husband, after studying medicine for a short time, and serving during the war for several years as an assistant surgeon in the army, and after settling for a short time on a farm at Carll Town in Hopewell Township, was in 1779 appointed Professor of Mathematics in the University of Philadelphia, and afterwards, by Mr. Jefferson, Director of the Mint. In 1819, he was chosen President of the American Philosophical Society, ending a long and honored career in 1824, at the age of 82. The writer well remembers him, having had the benefit of his instruction in mathematics and philosophy more than fifty years ago.

In 1794 James D. Westcott started a newspaper, which was called the *Argus*, and continued nearly two years. Afterwards his brother, John Westcott, tried another about 1803, but it did not succeed. In 1815 a political association, composed of Democrats, and called the Washington Whig Society, set up in opposition to a Washington Benevolent Society formed by the Federalists, established a paper called the *Washington Whig*, published at first by Peter Hay, Esq., now an Alderman in Philadelphia, who was by profession a printer. It has been ever since continued, under different names and under the patronage of different parties. In 1817 Mr. Hay sold to Wm. Shultz, who in 1821 sold to John Clark, during whose time the paper supported the administration of John Q. Adams. Clark sold in 1826 to J. J. McChesney.

In 1822 S. Siegfried started a second paper, called *The West Jersey Observer*. In 1824 he sold out to Robert Johnston, and in

1826 he purchased the *Whig* and consolidated them into one paper, called *The Whig and Observer*.

The Washington Whig was then revived, and after several changes, both being purchased by James M. Newell, he merged them in a new one, called *The Bridgeton Chronicle*, about 1837. He carried it on until his death in 1851, and different proprietors and editors have published it until the present time.

About 1846 another paper was started, called at first *The West Jersey Telegraph*, but it was soon changed to *The West Jersey Pioneer*, by which name it is still published. This paper and the *Chronicle* for several years have been conducted as neutral in politics.

In 1862 Fayette Pierson, who was connected with the *Washington Whig* in its early days, started the *Aurora*, now published as a democratic paper; so that there are three papers, where only one really good one can thrive, this being a case where, as in most of the towns of the State, too much competition has not tended to increase the value of the article produced.

As the early settlers of Bridgeton were mostly of Puritan lineage, there was always a disposition among them to encourage education. The first school of which any notice remains, was one kept by John Wescott in 1773, in which mathematics were taught. About the year 1792 Mark Miller, heir of Ebenezer Miller, deeded to trustees the lot on Giles Street for school purposes. In 1795 the Academy was erected on Bank Street, by a joint stock company, and for many years a good classical school was taught in it. Rev. Andrew Hunter, father of the present Gen. Hunter, taught a classical school in the town about the years 1780 to 1785. The public school-house on Bank Street was first erected in 1847. The number of youths between the ages of 5 and 16 in the township of Bridgeton, was then 540. In 1851, the number between 5 and 18 was 687. In 1862 there were between the same ages 917. The public school-house in Cohansey Township was built in 1848. Number of youths that year, 241. In 1853 the number was 301. In 1862 the number between the ages of 5 and 18 was 407. The school in Bridgeton employs 8 teachers, all females but one, and that in Cohansey one male and two females.

The Presbyterian Academy was built in 1852–53, and first opened in 1854. It is an incorporated body, governed by trustees elected by the Presbytery of West Jersey. There is, besides, an excellent school for young ladies, conducted by Mrs. Sheppard.

Cumberland Bank was first chartered in 1816, and commenced business in September of that year, with a capital of 52,000 dollars; James Giles, President, and Charles Read, Cashier. Giles died in 1816, and was succeeded by Daniel Elmer, and he having resigned in 1841, James B. Potter was appointed President. Mr. Read died in 1844, and was succeeded by the present Cashier, William G. Nixon. About 1857 the surplus earnings enabled the capital to be raised to 102,000 dollars, without the advance of any money by the stockholders; and so well has the institution been managed from the first, that it has always deserved and obtained the entire confidence of the community, and maintained its notes par with those of Philadelphia, often continuing to pay specie when the banks in the city could not. During the first fifteen years the deposits averaged about 20,000 dollars; then for the next fifteen they averaged about 30,000, while for the last fifteen they have averaged 50,000, often reaching 100,000 and 150,000 dollars. For the first thirty years there was a regular dividend of three per cent. half yearly, besides an extra dividend in 1844 of 24 per cent. Since that time 4, 4½, and 5 per cent. have been divided semi-annually. The surplus earnings, besides the regular dividends, have amounted to about 86,000 dollars, of which near 25,000 remains unappropriated.

Until within the last twenty years there were but few foreigners in the place, and they were persons born in Ireland or Scotland, who came to America in their youth. One young German who deserted from a Hessian regiment is remembered, who married and raised a large family. A very considerable number of Germans came into the county before the Revolution, and settled in the upper part of Hopewell, and in the adjoining part of Salem County, some of whose descendants took up their residence in Bridgeton. Most of these, it is believed, were glassblowers, who were employed to blow glass at the works early erected not far east of Alloways-town, said to have been one of the first established in America. Among these settlers was Jacob Fries, whose two sons, Philip of Friesburg, and John of Philadelphia, became men of considerable wealth. The writer remembers to have heard that when Independence was declared by the American colonies, old Jacob Fries was much concerned as to the possibility of getting along without a king, and advised that one should be brought over from Germany. That country, it is certain, has a plenty of rulers to spare, such as they are, but judging from the experience of the Grecians, it is doubtful whether one could be found worth a trial. An excellent teacher, a preceptor of the writer in his youth, was quite as much impressed with the impracticability of a republican government as Mr. Fries, and predicted that the writer would live to see a king inaugurated. The race of these doubters, it would seem, it not yet extinct.

About 20 years ago a German butcher, named Christian Cook, came to this place from Salem, and still carries on the business. Since his arrival, the number of families from different parts of Germany has so increased, that it is quite a common thing to hear the language in the streets, and the total number of that nation is not less than four or five hundred. They are in general an industrious, frugal race, and adopting a different usage from that which so long prevailed in Pennsylvania, by encouraging their children to learn and use the American language, it is hoped they will be a valuable addition to the population.

Most of the original settlers in the region called Cohansey, were Baptist or Presbyterian from the New and Old England, and happily their influence upon the religion and morals of the people was good, and is still apparent. Mr. Fithian enters in that journal, so frequently quoted, of the date June 26, 1776, while he was engaged in making a missionary tour up the Susquehanna River, in Pennsylvania: "I met on the road a tinker, on the way to what is called the new purchase. He has been at Cohansey, knows many there, at Pittsgrove, Deerfield, and New England Town. He told me that he had been acquainted in seven colonies, but never yet saw any place in which the inhabitants were so sober, uniform in their manner, and every way religious, as at New England Town, and Mr. Ramsey was his favorite preacher." While in Maryland he mentions a collection having been taken up, and says, "There were 34 pieces of silver in cut money." His summing up of this tour is, "Wherever I have been their character is mean, dishonest, and irreligious. A Jerseyman, and an impertinent every way troublesome scoundrel, seem to be words of nearly the same meaning." Under date of August 16, he writes: "I saw Mr. Farquar, a Scotch Presbyterian; he pronounced one sentence from his observation which is a most solid truth, and which I will record, ' I have discovered since my arrival that there are no slaves in America. but the Presbyterian clergy.'" In April, 1774, on his visit to Greenwich, after he had spent some months in Virginia, he enters, " The morning pleasant and Cohansie looks as delightsome as it used to be, and I went to meeting. How unlike Virginia. No rings of beaux, chattering before and after sermon on gallantry; no assembling in crowds after service to drive a bargain, no cool spiritless harangue from the pulpit; minister and people here, seem in some small degree to reverence the day; there neither do it." In the succeeding July, after his return, while residing as a tutor in the family of Mr. Carter, a wealthy gentleman, whose large mansion and possessions were on the west side of the Potomac in Westmoreland County, he enters : " A Sunday in Virginia don't seem to wear the same dress as our Sundays to the northward. Generally here by 5 o'clock on Saturday, every face, especially the negroes, looks festive and cheerful; all the lower class of people and the servants and slaves consider Sunday as a day of pleasure and amusement, and spend it in diversions. The gentlemen go to church to be sure, but they make that itself a matter of convenience, and account the church a weekly resort to do business."

Before dismissing this interesting journal, affording us so many glimpses of transactions in days long past, it may be interesting to make a few more extracts from it. His journey from home, on horseback, commenced October 20, 1773, when he left Greenwich by six, morning, rode to Michael Hoshel's, 8 miles, then to Quinton's Bridge, over toll bridge to Penn's Neck Ferry, then by North East to Baltimore. Then forded Patapsco to Bladensburgh, ferry at Georgetown, Alexandria, Colchester, ferry at Dumfries, Aquia, Stafford C. H., on the 28th arrived at Col. Carter's. Nomini Hall, Westmoreland, in all 260 miles, expense £3 6s. 6d. Returning next spring, he crossed the Potomac to Port Tobacco in Maryland, and then to Annapolis, and from there in a boat 25 miles to Rockhall, then to Chester Town and to Georgetown, Delaware. "Lodged at Mr. Voorhees; had evening prayers; since I left Cohansie have not heard the like. By Port Penn and Elsenborough to Greenwich. Stopt to see the forsaken Mrs. Ward." Her husband, Dr. Ward, had recently died. She was a Holmes, afterwards married Dr. Bloomfield, of Woodbridge, father of Gov. Bloomfield, and upon his death came to Bridgeton, where she died, quite aged. "Many had died the past winter—a very mortal winter." May 4,

" Last night fell a very considerable snow; 5th, last night was very cold, ice two inches thick; 6th, still very cold, the leaves on the trees are grown black, the fruit must be past recovery." In Virginia, he states, " the frost of May was very severe, killed the peaches, and in the upper counties the wheat and rye." 'May 11, " an ox killed to-day in Bridgeton which weighed upwards of 1000 lbs., supposed to be the largest ever killed in the county."

The poor of Cumberland have for a long time been mostly supported in a poor-house, situate about a mile and a half westwardly from Bridgeton. The question of having an establishment of this kind began to be agitated as early as 1799, but it was not until 1809 that Moore Hall and the property belonging to it was purchased. The present building was erected in 1852.

During the latter part of the last century it was quite common for persons in good circumstances to own one or two slaves, generally as house servants. Acts of the legislature passed as early as 1713 and from time to time until 1798 had sanctioned and regulated the owning and treatment of them. In 1804 an act was passed for the gradual abolition of slavery, which declared that those born after the 4th of July of that year should be held to service if a male until the age of 25 years, and if a female until the age of 21 years. After this some of those who were slaves for life, were manumitted. A few have remained nominally slaves until comparatively a recent period. The number in the county in 1790 was 120; in 1800 they had decreased to 75; in 1810 to 42; in 1820 to 28; in 1830 there were only two.

Very few newly-settled districts of country are healthy. The southern part of New Jersey was for many years an unhealthy region. Fever and ague were almost universal in the latter part of the summer and during the early part of the fall, generally disappearing after the nights became frosty. Until comparatively a recent period, scarcely a young person of either sex escaped the fever and ague. Every other day, and sometimes every third day, the person would be able to attend school or other avocation, but about the middle of the second or third day would be taken with a chill, which in the course of an hour or two would be followed by a hot fever. Often very violent intermittent or bilious fevers were epidemic. A healthy summer or fall was the exception and not the rule.

In a journal kept by Ephraim Harris, of Fairfield, who was born in 1732, and died in 1794, he enters: "That fatal and never to be forgotten year 1759, when the Lord sent the destroying angel to pass through this place, and removed many of our friends into eternity in a short space of time; not a house exempt, not a family spared from the calamity. So dreadful was it that it made every ear tingle, and every heart bleed; in which time I and my family was exercised with that dreadful disorder, the measles; but, blessed be God, our lives were spared." It is quite probable that the disorder here called measles, was in fact the smallpox.

Mr. Fithian enters in his journal under the date of July 4, 1774, when he was in Virginia: "We have several showers to day; the weather is warm, funky, very damp, and I fear will not turn out long to be healthful. With us in Jersey, wet weather about this time is generally thought, and I believe almost never fails being a·forerunner of agues, fall fever, fluxes, and our horse distempers." Under the date of August 9, 1775, when he was in Western Maryland, he enters: "News from below that many disorders, chiefly the flux (by which he means dysentery), are now raging in the lower counties, Chester, etc. I pray God Delaware may be a bar, and stop that painful and deadly disorder. Enough has it ravaged our poor Cohansians. Enough are we in Cohansey every autumn enfeebled and wasted with the ague and fever. Our children all grow pale, puny, and lifeless." The dysentery was very prevalent and fatal in Cumberland County in 1775, and again in 1806.

After the enlargement of the mill-pond east of Bridgeton, in 1809, and the raising of the new pond northward in 1814, intermittent and bilious fevers were common in Bridgeton for successive years. In 1823 these diseases prevailed to a fearful extent; but after this, in the course of three or four years, they ceased to prevail either in the town or other parts of the county. This improvement has been ascribed to more perfect draining, and to the use of lime for agricultural purposes. But while it is probable that these causes have had some effect, the change was too sudden, and has been too great to be ascribed mainly to them. Atmospheric, telluric, or other influences far more potent, must have occurred. What these are we do not know. The important fact, for which our people cannot be too thankful, is, that the providence of God has, for thirty years past, given us healthful seasons, instead of the sickness formerly so common. Our fall seasons are now as generally healthful as any other part of the year. In those years when the cholera was so fatal in many parts of the country, we were mostly exempt. Thirty years ago it could not be said with truth that Bridgeton was as healthy a place as most of the towns in the northern part of the State; but now this may be affirmed without fear of contradiction.

But little is known of the early physicians in Bridgeton or its vicinity. The first of whom there is any notice was Elijah Bowen, who, in 1738, was one of the founders of the church at Shiloh, and who had considerable practice afterwards in that vicinity. He was of the Baptist family, which settled and gave their name to Bowentown. After and partly contemporaneous with him was James Johnson from Connecticut, who was a practitioner as early as 1745, and appears to have resided near Bowentown, and died in 1759. It may be mentioned as characteristic of the habits of that time, that among the accounts of his executor are charges for wine for the use of the watchers, and of wine and rum for the funeral. After him was Dr. John Fithian, who in 1751 built the house on the south side of Broad Street, next above the residence of Charles E. Elmer, Esq. Dr. Jonathan Elmer commenced practice in 1768.[1]

---

[1] Jonathan Elmer was son of Daniel Elmer second; was born in 1745, and died in 1817. He was one of the first graduates of the Medical Department of the University of Pennsylvania, receiving the degree of M. B. (Bachelor of Medicine) in 1768, and of M. D. in 1771. In 1772 he was elected a member of the American Philosophical Society, of which Dr. Franklin was the President, and was considered the equal in medical knowledge of any physician in the United States. His health being infirm, he turned his attention more to politics, and was much in office until the change of parties in 1800. With all the family he was an ardent Whig, and entered earnestly into the measures of opposition to the encroachments of the British Government on the rights of the people of America. Although not a military man, he took a commission as commander of a company of militia, and was active in organizing measures of defence. He was one of the Committee of Vigilance, which, in fact, was for some time the governing power of the county; and in 1776 was a member of the Provincial Congress, and a member of the committee which framed the first constitution of the State. During most of the time the war lasted he was a member of Congress, and afterward one of the first senators. For many years he was the presiding judge of the Court of Common Pleas of the county, and was, in fact, a well-read lawyer. He became an elder of the Presbyterian church in Bridgeton. His descendants in the city are still numerous and highly respectable.

Ebenezer Elmer was a brother of Dr. Jonathan, was born in 1752, and died at the age of ninety-one in 1843. Having studied medicine with his brother, and when about to commence practice, the Revolutionary War broke out, and in January, 1776, he was commissioned as an ensign, and shortly after as lieutenant in a com-

He was probably the first regularly educated physician in the county, unless Dr. Ward of Greenwich, from Connecticut, who died young in 1774, may have been of that class. Dr. Thomas Ewing studied under Ward, and after practising a short time in Cape May, returned to Greenwich, and was an officer in the continental army. He died in 1782. His son, Dr. William B. Ewing, after a thorough education, settled as a physician in Greenwich in 1799. Dr. Elmer graduated in the newly-established medical school of Philadelphia as a Bachelor of Medicine in 1768, and in 1771 took the full degree of Doctor, his thesis in Latin having been printed. Dr. Rush said of him, that in medical erudition he was exceeded by no physician in the United States. He built, in 1772, a dwelling on the site of Charles E. Elmer's house; but being of feeble health, and not able to endure the long horseback journeys to which a physician was then exposed, he turned his attention to political life, received the appointment of sheriff, and was a member of Congress, and afterwards of the Senate. His brother Ebenezer commenced studying with him in 1773, and in 1775 began to visit patients in all parts of the county. He however entered the army at the breaking out of the Revolutionary War, and did not return to practice until it was over. In 1783, and for a few succeeding years, he was in full practice in Bridgeton and the neighborhood; but he soon became engaged in public life, and was afterwards only consulted in special cases and as a surgeon.

What physicians there were in other parts of the county, before the Revolution, is not known. There were probably very few. Jonathan Elmer, during the first year of his practice, appears to have gone to all parts of the county and more than once to the sea-

pany which soon joined the northern army; and in this capacity he served more than a year. During the remainder of the war he served as a surgeon, having been in service altogether seven years and eight months.

He was for a few years in business as a physician in Bridgeton, after the war, but soon relinquished it, and was much in public life as a member and Speaker of both branches of the legislature of New Jersey, a member of Congress, and supporter of Mr. Jefferson; collector of the customs, clerk, surrogate, and magistrate. In 1814 he commanded a brigade of militia called out for the defence of Philadelphia, and was usually known as General Elmer. In early life, as he has recorded in his journal, he "became a believer in the gospel plan of redemption by faith in Jesus Christ;" and afterwards was a member of the Presbyterian Church. He was the writer's father.

shore. In 1775 Ebenezer Elmer, then a student with him, visited Fairfield frequently to prescribe for the sick, and also Hopewell, Greenwich, and Deerfield. Dr. Otto, from Germany, who during the war lived in Gloucester County, and whose house and barn were burned by the British troops in March, 1778, and who was known as the Prussian Doctor, was called upon in difficult cases, not only in the neighborhood of his residence, but in other places in the adjoining counties of Salem and Cumberland.

Benjamin Champneys, a descendant of John Fenwick, studied with Ebenezer Elmer in 1793, and after a few voyages to sea married a daughter of Col. Potter, and settled as a physician in Bridgeton. He was much esteemed, but died young in 1814. Samuel M. Shute, who had been for a few years at the close of the war an officer in the army, studying medicine with Jonathan Elmer, and having married his daughter, was a leading physician until his death in 1816. They were succeeded by Isaac H. Hampton, whose father was a physician at Cedarville, but who commenced practice at Woodbury. He married a daughter of Gen. Giles and removed to Bridgeton in 1814, where he was in good practice until failing health obliged him to give it up about ten years ago. William Elmer, a son of Dr. Jonathan, commenced business as physician in 1812, but gave it up in 1817 upon the death of his father. He was succeeded by Dr. Ephraim Buck, Dr. William S. Bowen, and after some years the present Dr. William Elmer took a large share of the business. Besides these, there have been from time to time others, whose business was less extensive.

For some time after the formation of the county, the lawyers residing in Salem and in other parts of the State, were relied upon to transact the business. An old man named Husted told the writer many years ago, that when Geo. Trenchard, of Salem, was the king's attorney, and was examining him as a witness in a case of assault and battery, on trial in the Court of Quarter Sessions, he asked him several times how the accused struck him, and that having no better mode of explaining the matter he struck Mr. Attorney on the face and knocked him down. The lawyers in those days, as is still the practice in England, were required to stand up while they examined the witnesses. One of the Salem lawyers named Van Leuvnigh, who was very tall and slender, had the nickname of the Devil's darning needle. Samuel Leake, who was born in this county but resided in Trenton, and Lucius H.

Stockton often attended the courts here. Cortland Skinner, who was attorney-general at and before the Revolution, was in the habit of granting a nolle prosequi in petty cases, for a fee of half a joe, $8. Several are on file in the clerk's office.

Before the Revolution the judges wore gowns and wigs, and the lawyers wore gowns and bands, while in court. The sheriff, with as many justices and freeholders as he could conveinently summon, met the Justice of the Supreme Court, when he came into the county to hold a Circuit and Oyer and Terminer, which was commonly once in a year at the county line, on horseback, and escorted him to his lodging. This was the practice in England, and was required by the Governor's ordinance in this State. It was mentioned in the newspaper a few years ago, that one of the English Judges had fined the sheriff 100 pounds for neglecting this duty. The general introduction of railways has, however, abolished the practice in most cases. At the opening and closing of the court, from day to day, the sheriff and constables, with their staves of office, escorted the Judges from and to the tavern at which they dined, to the court-house, a practice which has been only recently abolished.

Courts of oyer and terminer and general gaol delivery were, until 1794, held by virtue of a special commission under the great seal, requiring, generally, two justices of the Supreme Court by name, the presence of one of whom was indispensable, and the county judges, and sometimes one or more justices of the peace by name, to hold the same for a number of specified days. Until 1845, the justices of the peace constituted the court of General Quarter Sessions of the peace, which had jurisdiction in all criminal cases, except those of a high grade. Judges of the Pleas were commonly also commissioned as justices; but only a small part of the justices were judges. For many years it was the practice for most of the justices, as well as the judges, to attend at least the first day of the term and dine together, all the court fees payable to them being appropriated to pay the expense, and in case these fell short, as was commonly the case, the justices were all assessed with their share of the balance, whether they attended or not.

The first attorney who is known to have settled in Bridgeton was Joseph Bloomfield, whose father was Dr. Bloomfield, of Woodbridge, the same who married the widow of Dr. Ward. The former

attended for a time a classical school kept by Rev. Enoch Green
in Deerfield. Having been admitted an attorney, he took up his
residence in Bridgeton about 1770. In the spring of 1776 he left
as captain of a company of soldiers. . He remained in the army
two or three years, and then resumed his profession, making Burlington his residence, where he married. In 1783 he was appointed
Attorney General. In 1801 he was elected Governor by the Democrats, and held the office, with the exception of one year when
there was a tie between the political parties, and the State was
without a Governor, until 1812, when he was appointed a Brigadier
General in the army. Richard Howell, of this county, became a
lawyer, and sometimes attended our courts, but did not reside in
the county. He was Governor from 1793 to 1801.

After the war James Giles, a young officer of artillery, attached
to the corps commanded at the close of the war by Lafayette, whose
father was an Episcopal clergyman, studied law, and having married a sister of Gov. Bloomfield, took up his residence in Bridgeton about the year 1787. In 1791 he built the house in which he
resided until his death in 1826. He transacted a large business as
an attorney for many years. In 1791 John Moore White commenced, and continued until 1808, when he removed to Woodbury,
where he resided until his death in 1862, at the age of 91. Daniel
Elmer was licensed in 1805; in 1808 married a daughter of Col.
Potter, and took up his residence for a short time in White's
deserted mansion. He had a large and lucrative business until
1841, when he was appointed one of the Justices of the Supreme
Court. About 1809 Isaac W. Crane came from Salem, and continued until 1839. Elias P. Seeley and Lucius Q. C. Elmer were
licensed in 1815. The former was Governor in 1832 and died. The
latter was appointed Attorney General in 1850, and in 1852 one of
the Justices of the Supreme Court. Henry T. Ellet practised law
here from 1833 to 1837, when he married a daughter of Governor
Seeley, and moved to Port Gibson, Mississippi, where he still resides.
James G. Hampton was licensed in 1839, and died in 1861. Charles
E. Elmer was licensed in 1842. In 1845 John T. Nixon was
licensed, and he, together with Charles E. Elmer, James R. Hoagland,
James J. Reeves, John S. Mitchell, Franklin F. Westcott, William
E. Potter, and J. Leslie Lupton, are now, in 1869, the lawyers of the
place.

But little is known of the military organization previous to the Revolution. Upon an old map of the farm lying on the west side of the road to Irelan's mill, as the mill now used for sawing staves was long called, and north of the run emptying into Jeddy's pond, there is laid down a lot of half an acre, about where the road to Shiloh now goes, marked as "town barracks." The precise meaning of this is now unknown.

The journal of Ebenezer Elmer, kept in 1775, shows that the county was alive with military preparations, especially after the news of the bloodshed at Lexington on the 19th of April. Companies were organized and officers chosen, and frequent drills took place. Richard Howell, afterwards Governor, raised the first company of one year men that left the county, by recommendation of the Committee of Safety, in October, 1775. Sunday, December 10, the entry is, "Went to meeting at Greenwich; Capt. Howell's soldiers there; came and went away in form. Coming home, Mr. Bloomfield proposed to me to send a petition to the Provincial Congress for himself Captain, Josiah Seeley 1st Lieutenant, and myself 2d, which was agreed to." The entry 13th of December is, "The soldiers went on board the Greenwich packet at evening, to sail for Burlington." 14th, "Cloudy day. The soldiers, captain, and all but eight or ten, went off in the dead of the night, on foot, to get clear of their creditors; their going aboard the vessel turned out only a sham."

It would seem from this last entry that Capt. Howell's men were, many of them, like those that gathered themselves unto David at the cave of Adullam, in distress, in debt, or discontented. The suspicions of the journalist, however, may not have been warranted by the facts. It appears from several previous entries that he had been desirous of procuring a commission in this company, and his disappointment may have produced his unfavorable surmises.

In the succeeding spring another company was raised, as proposed by Bloomfield, except that Josiah Seeley, having concluded to take a wife and stay with her, another person was commissioned as 1st Lieutenant, which marched for the northern frontier in March, 1776.

Several times during the Revolutionary War, fully half the militia of this county was in actual service. Col. Newcomb, of Fairfield, commanded a regiment, and so did Col. Potter. The latter was taken prisoner near Haddonfield, but was soon exchanged. John

Gibbon, the uncle of Mrs. Seeley, was also taken prisoner, and was among those who died on board the Jersey prison ship at New York. The British troops never reached this county.

During the war with Great Britain in 1814 a brigade of the militia of South Jersey was drafted, and encamped at Billingsport for the defence of Philadelphia, under the command of General Ebenezer Elmer, then the Brigadier General of the Cumberland Brigade. During the summer of that year the Poictiers, an English ship of the line, under the command of Sir John Beresford, lying in Delaware Bay, succeeded in breaking up the navigation as high up as the Cohansey. No serious engagements, however, took place between the hostile forces.

The inhabitants of Bridgeton suffered a terrible fright, which, alarming enough at first, in the end partook more of the ludicrous than the serious. To prevent boats from the enemy's ship coming up the river in the night, and plundering the town, a nightly guard was detailed and posted at a point on the river two or three miles from the town, but more than twice that distance by the water. All the vessels and boats passing the guard-house during the night were hailed and required to give an account of themselves. If an enemy appeared, a messenger was to be sent to a prudent officer at the town, who was intrusted with the duty, if needful, of giving the alarm by firing a cannon, and ringing the court-house bell, that being then the only bell in the place. About two o'clock of a midsummer night the gun was fired, and the bell rang with great animation. The scene that ensued may be imagined, but cannot easily be described, and great was the consternation. No one doubted that an enemy was close at hand. One or two persons threw their silver down the well. The militia, except some who as usual were among the missing, were assembled, and an attempt made to organize them for action. Happily, however, their prowess was not tested. The alarm, although not sounded until all doubt of its necessity seemed to be removed, turned out to be a false one, originating in the fright of a family near the guard-house, the head of which was absent, and in the fool-hardiness of the skipper of a small sloop, who took it into his head to pass the guard without answering their challenge, and who succeeded in bringing on himself and his crew a volley of musketry, and running the risk of being killed by a ball which passed directly over his head.

During the first quarter of the present century, the annual training day was the festival day next in importance to the fourth of July. The companies met for drill twice a year, and the regiments or brigades for inspection and review by the commanding general. On this latter day there was commonly a great turn out of men, women and children. Many evils grew out of the system, so that in South Jersey, although the law remained unaltered, after about 1830, the whole system fell into disuse. It is by no means certain, however, that the change has been for the better. The evils of the system, as happily is the case with most human affairs, were compensated by many advantages. The habit of bearing arms, and meeting for exercise, produced a spirit of self-reliance of no little consequence, while the holiday, which occurred on the day of the "great training," served to bring the people together and to cultivate kind and generous feelings, at a time when the means of intercourse were far more limited than they now are. It has been well remarked, in reference to the people of the Northern and Middle States, that the three things which had enabled them to carry on a republican government so successfully, were the congregational meetings and preaching on Sunday, the town meetings, and the training of the militia.

Bridgeton was incorporated as a city in 1865, with a Mayor and Common Council, and is divided into three wards, covering the territory of the former townships of Bridgeton and Cohansey. The number of inhabitants is estimated to be about 7,500.

CHAPTER IV.

MAURICE RIVER, MILLVILLE, AND LANDIS.

THE Indian name of the principal river running into Delaware
Bay was Wahatquenack, and there has been a tradition, which
like many other errors has passed into history, that its present
name Maurice, was derived from the circumstance that a vessel
called the Prince Maurice was burnt at an early date by the
Indians, in the reach since called, "No Man's Friend." Whatever
may be the truth, as to the burning of the vessel, while she was
repairing, according to one version of the story, it is much more
probable that the name was given to the river either by Mey, or
DeVries, captains of Dutch vessels, who visited the bay, the former
in 1623 and the other in 1631. A map of "*Nieuw Nederlandt,*"
published at Amsterdam in 1676, including New Jersey and *Zuyd
Revier,* or South River, as the Dutch called the Delaware, marks
very distinctly the entrance of Maurice River into the bay, and
names it *Mauritius Revier.* The same name, evidently the Dutch
or Latin name for Maurice, Prince of Orange, was given by some of
the Dutch writers to the Hudson. When the county of Cape May
was established by the legislature of West Jersey in 1692, they
bounded it on the east side of Morris River, so spelled in the printed
law. In the act of 1694 it is called Prince Morris' River. When
the county was set off from Salem, the law describing the township,
bounds it on Prince Maurice' River; but the township is called
Maurice River precinct.

In 1691 John Worlidge and John Budd, surveyors from Burlington, in the employment of the principal proprietors of West
Jersey, visited the streams on the lower part of the Delaware in a
vessel, and set off large surveys on both sides of Maurice River.
On the west side at the mouth they set off 10,000 acres for Wasse,
on the east side one of 20,000 acres for Robert Squibb, most of
which afterwards became the property of Thomas Byerly. Above
Byerly's survey, 2500 acres were set off for a town plot and called

Dorchester; it includes Leesburg, but no town was built or even commenced until more than a century afterwards. Above this was a survey to Bartlett, afterwards John Scott's, located for 10,000 acres, but containing more than double that quantity. All the early surveys contained many more acres than were returned.

But few permanent settlements were made on either side of Maurice River until after the formation of the county. There were, however, a sufficient number as early as 1720, to require the appointment of a constable "for Morris River," by the court of Quarter Sessions at Salem. Ten years after this one was appointed for the upper part and one for the lower. The old Cape Road, or as it was commonly called the King's Road, originally followed the Indian paths, crossing the Cohansey and Maurice Rivers above the tide, that is to say, the former at or near Bridgeton, and the latter about where the Union pond now is, thence across the Menantico at Leaming's mill, and the Manamuskin at the mill where Cumberland furnace was afterwards placed, now called Manamuskin Manor, and thence over Dennis' Creek swamp, near where the railroad now crosses the same. The mill afterwards owned by and called Leaming's mill, was built as early as 1720 by Rawson. Scott commenced selling parts of his tract, about this time, adjoining Manamuskin and Maurice River. The site of Port Elizabeth was sold probably about this time to John Purple.

Thomas Chalkley, a Friend from England, who married a sister of Jacob Spicer, states in his journal, 2d Month (April) 1726: "From Cohansey through the wilderness over Maurice River, accompanied by James Daniels, through a miry, boggy way in which we saw no house for about forty miles except at the ferry; and that night we got to Richard Townsend's at Cape May." Townsend lived in the upper precinct, not far from Tuckahoe, but where the ferry over Maurice River was, at which Chalkley crossed, is unknown; it was probably below Port Elizabeth.

A road was laid out in 1705, from Salem to Maurice River, which crossed Alloway's Creek at Quinton's Bridge, the Cohansey at Greenwich, thence to Henry Brooks' at Fairfield, then keeping the road by the meeting-house, on the bank of the river, at New England Town to Grimes' bridge (probably over Rattlesnake Run at Fairton,) then keeping the old road until it cometh to the road going to Daniel England's saw-mill, to two oak trees marked M. M. Daniel England's mill was at Buckshutem, and was afterwards called Carmack's mill.   It was probably this road that was travelled by Chalkley.   Although all the roads were originally laid out for six rods, or four rods wide, they were seldom opened, and until long after 1720 were only travelled on horseback.

Wasse's tract west of the river was not sold out in parcels until after 1738.   Prior to 1750, William Dollas, a Friend, purchased the land at the place since called Port Norris, and for many years a ferry was maintained there, this being one of the thoroughfares from Greenwich to Cape May, and may have been the ferry mentioned by Chalkley.

John Peterson, of Swedish origin, located the land where Mauricetown now is and settled there in 1730.   He laid surveys on several tracts in the neighborhood.   Subsequently Luke Mattox owned the property, and from him it was called Mattox landing, until about 1814, when three brothers named Compton became the proprietors, laid out the village of Mauricetown, and built several handsome dwelling-houses.   It is now a flourishing place, the principal inhabitants being engaged in the coasting and river trade, which although subject to occasional depressions, has been in the main prosperous.

The site of Dorchester was purchased by Peter Reeve just previous to 1800, and he laid out the town and commenced selling lots.   At that time there were but three houses in the vicinity.   A saw-mill had been erected at an early date.   Most of the original settlers here, as has been stated, were Swedes.   Some of them appear to have taken leases under the proprietors.   The names of Peterson, Lord, Errickson, Vanneman, Reagan (corrupted to Riggins) Hoffman, and others still remain.

Leesburg was established by two brothers named Lee, ship-carpenters from Egg-harbor, some time about the year 1800.   An old graveyard on the bank of the river, partly washed away, indicates that there were several settlers in the neighborhood at a much earlier date.   William Carlisle, now one of the wealthiest proprietors, went there in 1795, and found only two or three houses. It has been a place for building coasting vessels from the beginning.   In 1850 James Ward built a marine railway, and now there are two there, besides one at Dorchester.   Vessels are constantly on the stocks and undergoing repair at both these places. This region has advanced during the last year more perceptibly than any other part of the township.   There is much good land in the neighborhood, capable of great improvement as an agricultural district. The new railroad to Cape May passes through an uncultivated district, where, although most of the land is poor, there is much that is good, which it is believed will be settled and cultivated soon.

The bay shore and up the river for several miles was naturally a salt marsh. Above Port Norris it was banked and reclaimed at an early period. And it must be remembered that the first settlers established their farms on the banks of the streams, and depended on the natural marshes or embanked meadows for their hay. Laws were passed as early as 1760 for erecting banks by the joint efforts of the proprietors on the Cohansey. Until within the last thirty years, since when the introduction of lime and other fertilizers has enabled the farmers to raise hay of a better quality on their upland, the reclaimed meadows, notwithstanding the great expense generally attending the maintenance of the banks, were almost indispensable, and commanded a high price. Those on Maurice River, which are easily renovated by the muddy sediment deposited from the water when allowed to flow over them, are of an excellent quality, and are still of much value. The relative price, however, of upland and meadow land has undergone a considerable change, the former having risen and the latter depreciated in value.

About the year 1809 Messrs. Coates & Brinton commenced an embankment on the east side and near the mouth of Maurice River, about four miles in extent. In 1816 they extended their bank at great expense along the shore of the bay to East Creek, placing a dam at the mouth of West Creek, making a bank about fifteen miles long and inclosing several thousand acres of land. The promise of remuneration for this great outlay, which was never very encouraging, was entirely disappointed by the great storm of 1821, still remembered and spoken of throughout South Jersey as "the September Gale," which swept away the greater part of the bank. It occurred on the first Monday of September, nomination day for members of Assembly, and blew down and injured much of the woodland in the county. Many of the Lombardy poplars, then very common around our dwellings, were blown down, but this proved to be no loss, the tree, although for a time very popular, not being desirable for any purpose. No attempt to repair the bank was made until 1849, when Gen. Cadwallader, of Philadelphia, who had been owner of the property, inclosed about 1200 acres, at the mouth of the river, which are now of much value.

Besides the natural oyster beds near the mouth of the river, this product of the waters has been greatly increased, by planting them in the cove. These oysters are esteemed the best that are found in the Delaware, owing no doubt to the fact that the water which flows out of the river has in it much vegetable sediment upon which they live and fatten. The proper habitation of a good oyster is where the salt water of the ocean is diluted by fresh water from an inland stream, bringing with it a sufficient supply of vegetable matter. A very considerable business employing many small sloops and schooners, has grown out of the planting, gathering, and carrying to market of oysters produced in Delaware Bay, which is susceptible of great increase, and would undoubtedly be far more advantageous to the citizens of this State, if the property of the soil under the water, suitable for producing them, could become private property. The tenacity with which the privilege of holding a right to common property in the upland and in the water has been held not only in this country, but in Europe, although perhaps natural enough, has always proved detrimental to the community. Those commons which were adjacent to all the villages in England, and which it cost years of conflict to divide by means of inclosure acts, have entirely disappeared to the great benefit of the people. And it cannot be doubted that the many thousand dollars expended by this State, in obtaining the decision of the Supreme Court of the United States, in the case of Martin *vs.* Waddell, decided in 1842 that the land under the navigable waters of the State is public property up to high water mark, and does not belong to the proprietors, was sadly misspent. Happily, however, the whole subject is in the power of the legislature, and will some time be properly regulated. The right of private property, as human nature is constituted, is indispensable to induce an energetic and profitable use of the land, whether covered with water or susceptible of cultivation, and suitable for the habitation of man.

The present site of Port Elizabeth was purchased of John Scott by John Purple, about the year 1720. The land on the west side of the Manamuskin was purchased by different persons soon after. Among the purchasers was John Hoffman, who made the deed for the property on which the Swedes church was erected. The grand-

father of the late Jonathan Lore purchased and moved on to his
farm about the year 1750.   At that time he owned the only horse
on the creek, and there was but one ox.   He built a barn which is
still standing, the frame of which was cut and hewed at Antuxet
and floated down to the bay and to Maurice River, and thence up
to the farm.   When it was raised, it being about 25 by 40 feet in
size, the people assisting said there never would be enough hay
cut on the river to fill it.   In 1771 John Bell, who had become the
owner of the property, sold it to Mrs. Elizabeth Clark, afterwards
Bodley, from whom the name of the place originated.   A dam was
put across the mouth of the Manamuskin, for the sake of the
valuable meadows above before 1782, in which year a law was
passed authorizing it.   Mrs. Bodley laid out the town about the
year 1785.   When in that year the act of Congress was passed
establishing districts for the collection of the duties imposed on
imported goods, the eastern side of the Delaware from above Camden to Cape May was constituted the district of Bridgeton, and the
towns of Salem and Port Elizabeth on Maurice River were made
ports of delivery.   All vessels requiring a license, the owners of
which reside in this district, are required by the laws to letter them
as belonging to one of these places, or to Bridgeton, which is the
only port of entry.   For a few years after this act was passed there
was some trading out of Maurice River and the Cohansey to the
West Indies; but for the last thirty years or more, this has entirely
ceased.   The tendency of canals, railroads and other modern improvements, is to concentrate trade in the great marts of business,
where there are greater facilities for carrying it on.

The road from Port Elizabeth to Tuckahoe was laid and opened
in 1796.   In the year 1794 an act of the legislature appointed
commissioners to lay out and open roads from Bridgeton to
Cooper's Ferry, as Camden was then designated, and also from
Roadstown and from Port Elizabeth to Bridgeton.   These commissioners laid these roads, but only that from Roadstown to
Cooper's Ferry was opened.   That from Port Elizabeth to Bridgeton passed through Buckshootem, but it was never opened.   One
nearly in the same place was afterwards laid in the usual manner.

Joshua Brick, a son of John Brick, a prominent citizen of the
county, who at one time owned what are now Sheppard's and
Wood's mills, went to Maurice River about 1795.   He, and his
son Joshua, who died at an advanced age in 1860, were leading

inhabitants of Port Elizabeth, especially the son. He laid out the town called Bricksborough, and sold lots there in 1807. Neither place, although they are well situated for trade, has attained the importance that was expected. They may indeed be characterized as decayed villages. There is no reason, however, to doubt that they will hereafter greatly improve.

James Lee, of Irish descent, removed to this place from Chester County, Pennsylvania, about the year 1797, and in 1801 his half-brother Thomas came. James, who was an active enterprising man, too spasmodic in his efforts to succeed well, established glassworks in connection with Philadelphians, near where they still remain, in the year 1801. They made window glass. He did not, however, long remain an owner, having after a few years engaged in works at Millville and at Bridgeton. About 1817 he removed to the west, and died at New Orleans. In 1816 the glassworks at Port Elizabeth were purchased by a company of Germans, of whom the Getsingers were prominent members, who carried them on nearly thirty years. About 1813 works were erected on the east side of Manamuskin, just south of the road, which were carried on several years, but have long since been taken down. About 1830 glassworks were established at Marshallville, in the extreme eastern corner of the township, on the Tuckahoe River, and are still continued.

One of the well known citizens of this place was Dr. Benjamin Fisler, who died at the advanced age of eighty-five in 1854. His father and mother were natives of Switzerland. Their eleven children were remarkable for their longevity, one only dying at forty-five, the others from seventy-three to ninety-three, and the aggregate of their ages amounting to 883 years. The Doctor was admitted as a preacher among the Methodists in 1791, and was for a time a missionary in Nova Scotia. He settled in Port Elizabeth in 1798, and was the leading and most of the time the only physician of the place for about fifty-five years, being at the same time a very acceptable local preacher. His descendants are quite numerous, but none of them remain at the old homestead. Thomas Lee married his sister.

The first tavern stood near the creek, just below Oglee's store. The present tavern house was built in 1803.

In 1830 the present truss-bridge over the Manamuskin was built by the Board of Freeholders.

The districts of country bordering on the Menantico and Manamuskin, the most important tributaries of Maurice River, were
originally covered with pine and other trees, and produced much
good lumber for market. Saw-mills were erected on these streams
at an early day. Eli Budd, who was originally of the family of
Friends of that name in Burlington County, but who became a
Methodist as early as 1785, in this year purchased the property at
the head of the Manamuskin, and afterwards put up a forge for
manufacturing iron. About 1810 his son Wesley, in company
with one or more persons in Philadelphia, established a blast-
furnace at the place now called Manamuskin Manor, formerly Cumberland Furnace. In 1818 they failed, and the property went into
new hands. Subsequently the iron manufacture was profitably
maintained at this place by Edward Smith, of Philadelphia, and
continued until 1840, when the coal on about 15,000 acres of land
connected with the establishment, being entirely consumed, the
business was abandoned, and the works went to decay. The large
transportation of ore and other materials consumed, and of the iron
manufactured, was carried on by the channel of Menantico Creek
up to Schooner Landing, and thence by the ordinary road. A
furnace was established on the Tuckahoe River about 1820, but
did not long continue in use.

For the first forty or fifty years of this century the production
of iron in blast furnaces was a very important branch of business
in the southern part of New Jersey. The ore used was principally
what is called bog ore, much of which was dug in the swamps of
Downe Township, and other parts of the county, and in Gloucester
and Burlington Counties. It appears to have been iron held in
solution by water, and deposited during a long succession of years
in the sand or mud of low places. The quantity found in this
county was not large, and was soon exhausted. Afterwards the
ore was brought from the State of Delaware, and from Burlington
County. It was smelted by the use of lime as a flux, either in
the shape of oyster-shells or of stone-lime, and was of so good a
quality as to be run directly from the furnace into stove and other
castings. The stoves used in Philadelphia, the northern part of
New York, and in the Eastern States, were to a large extent made
in New Jersey. What could not be made into castings, was run
into pigs; but this was only an inconsiderable portion of the
whole. As the charcoal used was the most bulky and most im-

portant article, the ore was taken to the places where this was produced. The manufacture of iron in this manner is believed to have entirely ceased. Castings are now made almost exclusively by melting pig and other iron, in what are called cupola furnaces.

Schooner Landing, on the Menantico, about a mile below where the railroad crosses that stream, was at one time a place of considerable business. The road from Millville to Port Elizabeth passed through here originally. In the year 1793, Fithian Stratton, afterwards well known as an energetic but eccentric Methodist preacher, purchased the property, and in 1800 laid out a town of considerable size, which he called "Stratton Burrough," the last part so spelled for borough. He made efforts to have a bridge over Maurice River, west of the place, and a direct road to Bridgeton; hoping thus to get ahead of Millville. The project however failed, and although some dozen houses were erected, they have all been removed, the borough has disappeared, and the name passed into oblivion. The bridge over the creek was abandoned and sold, and the road vacated. This was the result of the final establishment, after a long contest, of the present straight road, and the bridge over the Menantico, not far from its mouth, which was completed in 1820.

There was no town at the place now called Millville, until after the commencement of the present century. Until 1756 the road travelled from Cohansey Bridge to Maurice River Township and Cape May, called—as the roads laid out by the public officers usually were—the King's highway, passed over Chatfield branch, at a dam made by the beavers, and still known as Beaver Dam, where, in the olden time, there was a tavern, and thence across Maurice River, above the tide, a little below the entrance of Lebanon branch, and thence across the Menantico at Leaming's Mill. Some time before 1754 a bridge had been built over Maurice River where this king's highway crossed, which, at the May term of this year, was presented by the grand jury as a nuisance for being out of order; and the Court of Oyer and Terminer, Mr. Justice Neville presiding, ordered the township of Maurice River to pay a fine of ten pounds, unless it was repaired by the next term. Shortly after, and probably in consequence of this proceeding, a public road was laid from Berriman's Branch, near Leaming's Mill, to Shingle Landing, on the east side of the river, a little below the present bridge; and a bridge, resting on log cribs, was built over the river. In 1756 a road was laid from this new bridge, commencing at Lucas Peterson's house, supposed to have been the house on the west side of the river, afterwards kept as a tavern, to the beaver dam, which soon superseded the old King's highway, now entirely disused and forgotten. After this, for many years, the place was called the New Bridge.

Prior to 1790, Henry Drinker, Joseph Smith, and others, forming a company called the Union Company, had purchased 24,000 acres of land, comprising the principal part of the 19,563 acres survey laid for Thomas and Richard Penn, and of their 6000 acres survey, and of several small surveys to other persons. The site of Millville is on the first-named survey. This company put up the dam, and raised the pond still known as the Union Mill Pond, and established mills. Large floating-gates were put in this dam, and since maintained for floating down the lumber; and until the last twenty years a considerable quantity was taken to market in that way.

In 1795 the Union property was purchased by Eli Elmer, Joseph Buck, and Robert Smith, and they sold one-twelfth part to Ezekiel Foster. Joseph Buck, who had been sheriff of the county, soon removed from Bridgeton to Maurice River Bridge, where he died in 1803. He laid out the town, and called it Millville, the object being to bring the water from the Union pond, and to establish the mills and other works on the banks of the river. This plan, however, was not then carried out. In 1801 the township was set off by law as it remained until Landis Township was formed.

The tavern-house at the northeast corner of Main and High Streets was built by Mr. Buck for his residence, but was not used as a tavern until several years afterwards. A house on the west side of the river, near the bridge as it then existed, with a considerable tract of land, was owned by Alexander Moore, of Bridgeton, and in this a tavern was kept. In 1813, when it was owned by his grandson, Alexander T. Moore, a law was passed authorizing him to dam the river at that place, but the work was never commenced. At a later date a law was obtained to authorize the construction of a navigable canal from Malaga, but the project shared the same fate as the other.

The tavern-house at the northwest corner of Main and High Streets was built by Bernard M'Credy, about 1811. After the death of Mr. Buck, his executors sold the lots of the town as he had laid it out, of which, however, no authentic record is known to exist. So slight was the prospect then considered that the town would increase, that several of the purchasers neglected to take their deeds, and so the property remaiued for more than thirty years, until his heirs claimed, took possession of, and disposed of it. In 1858 a survey and map of the town were completed under the directions of the township committee, and in March, 1859, a law was enacted, that, upon the map being filed in the clerk's office, showing the location of the different streets, they should become public highways.

Union Mill, and much of the land originally belonging to the company, became the property of Thomas Stone, and in 1806 was purchased by Keyser & Gorgas. In 1813 they sold to James Lee and others, and they to Smith & Wood, of Philadelphia. The firm of Smith & Wood commenced the extension of the canal, which had been previously begun, and brought down the water, and erected a blast furnace, which for a time they carried on. In 1822 Smith sold out, and the property was owned and carried on by David C. Wood until 1850, when it and the appurtenant tracts of land, comprising near twenty thousand acres, became the property of Richard D. Wood, of Philadelphia. Iron castings continued to be made until about 1849, when the manufacture of iron directly from the ore was discontinued. The annual product was about 600 tons.

Two large establishments for smelting and moulding iron from the pigs have been substituted, at which very heavy castings are made, the whole annual product being from four to five thousand tons.

The canal having been enlarged, a cotton mill was put in operation in 1854, at a cost of about 250,000 dollars. There are over 18,000 spindles, 430 looms, employing 350 hands, to whom wages are paid exceeding sixty thousand per annum. The average monthly product is about 160,000 yards of cotton cloth, which may be largely increased. The main building is 280 feet long four stories in height, lighted with gas, which it is proposed shortly to introduce into the town.

About the year 1806 James Lee and others started a glass manufactory above the bridge, and afterwards the business was continued by successive firms. For several years window glass was made, but for some thirty years past the establishment made only hollow ware. In 1832 the works at Schetterville, south of the town, were commenced, and made window glass until 1854, since which time only hollow ware has been made. The two ·establishments are now carried on by one firm, who produce annually glass of the value of 250 to 300 thousand dollars. Until within the last three or four years these works used only wood, of which, of course, large quantities were consumed. Now much the largest proportion of the fuel is coal, the annual consumption being about 4000 tons, and 1500 cords of wood. There are six furnaces in all, of which five are kept in operation, producing about 4000 dozen bottles daily. About 150 tons of sand, 95,000 pounds of soda ash, 1250 bushels of lime, and 150 bushels of salt, are used monthly. A manufactory of flint glass ware is in the process of erection.

Contemporaneous with the introduction of glassworks was the discovery of immense beds, or rather banks, of fine sand on the west side of the river, from two to five miles below the town. This is of so good a quality that besides the domestic consumption, from eight to ten thousand tons are annually exported to Boston and other places.

Until 1807 the bridge was without a draw for the passage of masted vessels. In that year a new one was built, containing a draw or hoist, a little above the site of the original structure, the timber and other materials of which were sold. In 1816 it was found necessary to build a new bridge, and considerable effort was made to have it placed so as to conform to the main street of the town, but after much contention the Board of Freeholders decided to build on the old site. So imperfect was the structure, that in 1837 a new one was found necessary, and a law having been obtained for the purpose, and the road on the west side being laid to conform, it was put as it now stands, in a line with the street. This bridge as well as that over the Cohansey being much used and having until recently been badly constructed, have been very expensive affairs. The existing bridge was finished in 1861.

The site of the town was a sandy knoll, so that the roads through it were always bad except a short time when frozen, and the sidewalks were unpleasant, until by the aid of clay and gravel they have been made good. While swing wells were in use a bet was made that an excavation large enough to hold a barrel could not be filled by drawing water and pouring it from the bucket from sunrise to sunset; a wager, the unlucky operator of the swing was glad to acknowledge he had lost long before the set time expired. Until after the commencement of this century, there were not more than five or six houses in the neighborhood of the bridge. This being the head of navigation, the same causes that produced a town at Cohansey bridge operated here. Large tracts of land covered with wood and timber had only this outlet to market. Until the erection of the furnace and the glass-house, almost the only employment of the people in this vicinity was the cutting and carting of wood, and taking it to Philadelphia, then the only market accessible. This business still continues to a considerable extent, but the prosperity of the place is no longer dependent on it, the business of manufacturing iron castings and glass, and more recently cotton, being far more important and productive. The population, for many years, increased very slowly. In 1840 there were about 1000 inhabitants, in 1850 about 1500, and in 1860 about 3200, and they are rapidly increasing. Up to 1815 the stage route to Philadelphia was by the way of Bridgeton, since then by Malaga, and for several years there had been a daily line, until the railroad to Glassboro, brought into use in 1860, directed the travel in that direction. In 1863 the railroad to Cape May was opened.

A steamboat to Philadelphia was started by a joint stock company in 1846; but the route was found too long, and the business proving unprofitable was soon abandoned. Recently a steam-propeller has commenced running regularly to New York, making nearly a trip each week, and carrying the various manufactures of glass at Glassboro and Millville, as well as other articles to that great market. Considerable capital is also invested in the coasting trade, the vessels engaged in it coming to the place for repairs and to winter. The country around, not being naturally very productive, and remaining until recently unimproved, the supply of provisions was, for many years, by no means abundant, but with increased demand, the supply has also increased, until there is now, by the aid of easy access to Philadelphia, no deficiency. The health of the place, which was once by no means good, has greatly improved.

In 1857 a bank with $50,000 capital commenced, which at the end of the first year reported $10,000 deposits, and now $100,000, although the large manufacturers make but little use of it. The institution is well managed, and makes regular half-yearly dividends.

A town hall was erected in 1856, affording good accommodation for public meetings, lectures, and concerts.

The graveyard, at the corner of Second and Sassafras Streets, dates back to the commencement of the settlement. About 1800 a house was erected on this lot which was used as a school-house, and for religous services, the different denominations worshipping there, the Presbyterians having preaching perhaps more statedly than the others. The Rev. Abijah Davis, of that denomination, who resided in the township, published a new version of the Psalms, and was no mean poet, and wrote a good deal for the newspapers over the signature of Happy Farmer, ranking among the earnest supporters of the Democratic administration, was accustomed to hold service there for several years pretty regularly. The first meeting-house erected was that at the corner of Second and Smith Streets, commenced for a dwelling, but converted into a house for religous worship by the Methodists in 1822. It was rebuilt in 1845. The Presbyterian house on Second Street was built in 1838, and enlarged in 1855. The Baptist house on the same street in 1843. In 1858 a second Methodist church was finished on McNeal Street, in the northwestern part of the town. In 1862 the Catholics erected a chapel in the same neighborhood. Preparations are making to build an Episcopal church; stated worship is maintained in all the houses; and there is besides a Protestant Methodist society which holds its meetings at Schetterville, but has as yet no house.

The public school-house on Sassafras Street was completed in the year 1849. In 1832 the number of scholars returned was 124. In 1863 the number was 1648. There are now three houses occupied. The number taught in the first named, by a male principal, and six female assistants, was 394. The new house, known as the Furnace School, is situate on Dock Street. There are three teachers who had in 1863 an average attendance of 124 pupils. There is also a public school on Second Street, in the southern part of the town, at the place commonly called Schetterville, with two teachers and 60 pupils. It thus appears that a little more than one-half the youth of a suitable age are under tuition.

Millville was incorporated as a city with a Mayor and Common Council in 1866, and three wards, comprising all the township which remained after the setting off of Landis. The city has since

7

rapidly increased in business and population.   The inhabitants in 1869 are estimated to number 5600.

Charles K. Landis, Esq., became the proprietor of a large tract of the land in the upper part of Millville Township, and extending into the adjoining counties of Gloucester and Atlantic, and commenced selling to settlers in October, 1861.   The inhabitants then residing on his purchase probably did not number fifty, and on the whole of what was set off as Landis Township did not exceed two hundred.   He laid out a town situate on both sides of the railroad to Glasboro, about two and a half miles east of Maurice River, and about seven miles north of Millville City, which he called Vineland.   The first house was erected in February, 1862, on Landis Avenue, which has been recently purchased by the Vineland Historical Society, and removed to Peach Street, to be preserved as a memento of Vineland's commencement.   A post office was established upon the condition that Mr. Landis should pay twenty dollars a quarter for carrying the mail, which he continued to do for nearly two years.   The office was kept at the residence of Andrew Sharp, the only good house then in the tract, situated at the corner of Park Avenue and Main Road.   The receipts for the quarter ending September 30, 1862, were $8.50.   They have since exceeded two thousand dollars per quarter.   Roads were extensively opened, so that there are now on the whole tract about one hundred and sixty miles.   At Christmas, 1862, it is stated by a recent historian of the settlement, that such progress had been made that "seventy-five settlers and one fiddler could be rallied at a Christmas festival."

An Episcopal church and academy were erected in 1863, and a considerable number of private dwellings.   Emigration became brisk, so that by January, 1864, one thousand acres of land had been sold.   This was mainly the result of an extensive system of advertising by means of a weekly sheet called *The Vineland Rural* and other publications, whereby the real and supposed advantages of the location for a prosperous settlement were made known throughout the Northern and Eastern States.

In March, 1864, a law was passed setting off more than half the township of Millville into a new township, to be called the township of Landis.   This law embodies most of the peculiar features of the system adopted by the founder, which it is believed have aided very materially in promoting its rapid growth and its continued prosperity.

Besides the usual powers of the inhabitants and officers of the townships in New Jersey, this act gives authority to the township committee to appoint overseers of roads and authorizes the election of one superintendent of roads, with a salary, whose powers are very ample, and who is required to have work on the roads done by contract. The side of the roads in front of all improved lands, are required to be seeded in grass within two years, and kept clear of noxious weeds; and shade trees are to be planted at such distances apart as the committee shall direct. The committee may require all buildings to be set at a distance not exceeding seventy-five feet from the side of the road outside of Vineland, and not exceeding twenty feet in the town. These powers have been exercised to the great benefit of the settlement, adding very much to its symmetry and beauty. The roads called avenues are 100 feet in width, and have generally two rows of trees, mostly maples, but in some cases fruit trees on each side, while the other roads are from 50 to 66 feet in width with one row of trees on each side, the road-beds for carriages being thirty feet in width. No person is required to inclose his ground with a fence, no cattle, sheep, or swine being allowed to run at large. The absence of fences and inclosures about the dwellings is a marked feature of the place, causing it to present as yet a naked appearance to eyes accustomed to these hitherto indispensable incumbrances, but when the hedges and ornamental trees and shrubbury which are being very generally planted shall have time to grow, this absence will no doubt be found to be a great improvement.

The law also provides that no ale, porter, beer, or other malt liquor shall be sold as a beverage, except at a regularly licensed inn or tavern; and that it shall be submitted to the people annually at their regular town meeting, to decide whether they shall apply to the court for a license for an inn or tavern to sell intoxicating liquors as a beverage in the township, and that no license shall be granted unless a majority of the votes shall be in favor of the same. The result has been that no license has been granted, and at the last annual town meeting the vote against a license was unanimous.

Two other rules were adopted by Mr. Landis in making most of his sales, which, it is supposed, have materially aided his design.

One is that he has sold his farm lands in small parcels, of from five to fifty acres each, and most generally not exceeding fifteen acres, so that the engrossment of the soil by speculators other than the proprietor himself has been prevented, persons of small means have been enabled to purchase, and the number of settlers has been largely increased. Another is that a full title to the land is not made until the purchaser has erected a dwelling, cleared up and cultivated a certain portion of his land, usually two and a half acres, and made the required roadside improvements. The combined influence of these measures, the extensive advertisements of the scheme, the favorable reports of invited visitors engaged in agricultural clubs and in writing for the newspapers, and the real advantages of the place, especially to persons whose residence was in the Northern and Eastern States, and whose liability to lung or other complaints, or other causes, made a change to a milder and dryer climate advisable, caused a rapid growth, probably unsurpassed in any place outside of a commercial centre like Chicago or other cities in the United States, which have astonished the world.

Most of the land comprised in Mr. Landis's tract could have been purchased ten years ago at from two to ten dollars an acre, according to the growth of timber it contained. Now the unimproved town lots, having 50 feet front and 150 feet deep, sell for $150, and some on Landis Avenue have sold at $40 a foot front, while much of the improved land sells at $150 to $200 an acre. A large population has collected, and many very handsome dwellings have been erected, so that the town is selected by many persons possessed of means as a most desirable residence. Good church buildings have been erected by the Episcopalians, Presbyterians, Methodists, and Baptists, who have stated preaching and a good attendance, and there are besides, Unitarians, Second Adventists, and Friends of Progress, who have organized societies. Two weekly newspapers are published. Education has been carefully provided for, there being now fourteen public schools in the township, and an academy for the higher branches. The Methodist society has located its seminary for South Jersey at this place, and have commenced a fine building estimated to cost about $75,000. Various manufactures have been established, operated by steam power, and much activity prevails. A leading object of the settlers has been to cultivate fruits, for which the soil and climate are supposed to be peculiarly favorable. While it cannot be affirmed that these efforts have been always successful, it is certain that there has been a large production of berries, grapes, and peaches, and a considerable amount of sweet potatoes and tomatoes. The number of inhabitants in Landis Township at this time (1869) may be estimated to be 6500. On the whole tract of Mr. Landis in the three counties there are probably 10,000 inhabitants.

The area of Cumberland County is stated in the recent geological survey of the State to be as follows:—

Townships.	Tide Marsh.	Total.
Bridgeton	....	9,849 acres
Deerfield	21,517 acres	26,656 "
Downe	14,176 "	57,043 "
Fairfield	....	48,192 "
Greenwich	4,410 "	11,360 "
Hopewell	1,875 "	19,200 "
Landis	....	46,522 "
Maurice River	7,174 "	67,559 "
Millville	1,158 "	32,224 "
Stone Creek	768 "	11,475 "
Totals	51,078 "	330,080 "
Area of the whole State . .	295,474 "	4,849,069 "

Prior to 1851 there was no attempt to assess taxes upon the tax payers in proportion to the value of their property. But in that year such a system was commenced, and with some variations has been since continued. The values returned by the assessors of the several townships have been as follows:—

Townships.	1852.	1860.	1865.	1868.
Cohansey . . .	$300,000	$401,000	....	....
Bridgeton . . .	900,000	850,000	$2,279,000	$2,303,000
Deerfield . . .	443,000	500,000	742,000	773,000
Downe	580,000	657,000	681,000	715,000
Fairfield . . .	705,000	875,000	1,059,000	1,000,000
Greenwich . . .	556,000	571,000	631,000	656,000
Hopewell . . .	561,000	686,000	1,000,000	1,200,000
Landis	......	......	650,000	800,000
Maurice River . .	538,000	575,000	673,000	750,000
Millville . . .	620,000	870,000	1,148,000	1,681,000
Stone Creek . . .	342,000	550,000	550,000	572,000
Totals . .	5,545,000	6,535,000	9,913,000	10,450,000

CHAPTER V.

RELIGIOUS DENOMINATIONS.

THE first organized church in this region of which there is any authentic record was the old Cohansey Baptist Church, although it is believed the Cohansey Presbyterian Church in Fairfield was cotemporaneous, if not earlier. Many Baptists and Presbyterians came into the county together from New England and Long Island. Morgan Edwards, who was from Wales, and is mentioned in Sabine's History of the American Royalists, published a History of the New Jersey Baptists in 1789, which is now a rare book. He states that "about the year 1683, some Baptists from Tipperary, Ireland, settled in the neighborhood of Cohansey; in 1665, arrived Obadiah Holmes, from Rhode Island. About this time Thomas Killingsworth settled not far off, which increased the number to nine souls, and probably as many more including the sisters; the above nine, with Killingsworth, formed a church in the spring of 1690. The Baptist church from which it sprung in Tipperary, called Cloughkatier, was flourishing in 1767 when I visited it."*

"In 1710 the Rev. Timothy Brooks, and his company, united with this church; they had emigrated hither from Massachusetts, about 1687, and had kept a separate society for 23 years, on account of difference in opinion relative to predestination, singing psalms, laying on hands, &c." He continued to be the pastor until his death in 1716. As early as 1702 he purchased 107 acres of land at Bowentown, comprising the farm on which the brick house on the hill stands, which was afterwards conveyed to the trustees of the Cohansey Baptist Church, and held as their parsonage until 1786, when it was sold to David Bowen, and was for several years the residence and property of Ebenezer Elmer. It is said there was a meeting-house, erected and occupied by Brooks' society,

* Rev. Mr. Wright, in his recent historical sketch of the Roadstown Baptist Church, says Cloughketin (as he spells it) Church was still in existence in 1838.

opposite the parsonage, which stood a few rods south of the road, about forty rods west of the brick house, and was still in use within the writer's memory.

In 1711 Edwards says, the society put up a building on the lot afterwards occupied, a little east of Sheppard's mill, South Hopewell. It is supposed, however, that this is a mistake. The Baptists about this time built a log house in that part of Fairfield called Back-Neck, the graveyard attached to which is still visible, and it is most probable that this is the house he refers to, for he says the title proved defective and the tradition is that there was no little difficulty in fixing upon the proper location in 1741.

At this time a new wooden church building was erected on the ground south of the road leading east from Sheppard's mill, where the old graveyard still remains. One of the stones has on it this inscription. "In memory of Deborah Sweeney, who departed this life the 4th day of April, 1760, in the 77th year of her age. She was the first white female child born in Cohansey." Edwards says, this house was 32 by 36 feet and "had a stove." By this is meant that it had a stove when he wrote in 1789, and this was so unusual as to claim special mention. Very few churches in this region, were warmed with fires until after the commencement of the present century, and they were not then introduced without much opposition from old people, who thought them needless, if not dangerous. For many years a stove was not to be had; and open fireplaces, which were alone used in dwellings, were not suitable for a church. After stoves were introduced, so long as wood continued to be burned, that is to say until about twenty or twenty-five years since, they did not comfortably warm the buildings, it being common for females to have footstoves in their seats. It is also to be noticed that most of the early churches were built near to running streams, for the purpose of enabling those who attended to procure water for themselves and their horses. It was common for the minister to hold two services on the Sunday, with an intermission of an hour or half hour; a practice which was continued at Fairfield within the memory of the writer. The old frame house remained until after 1804, about which time the new brick church was erected at Roadstown, to which the congregation removed.

Brooks was succeeded by William Butcher, who died in 1724, and was succeeded by Nathan Jenkins from 1730 to 1754. Robert Kelsay, from Ireland, came to Cohansey in 1738, became a Baptist in 1741, and pastor in 1756, dying in 1789. He frequently, if not statedly, preached in the court-house at Cohansey Bridge, where there was no organized church of any denomination until forty-five years after it became the county town. Henry Smalley succeeded him and died in 1839. The particulars of the various churches in the county it is not proposed to continue longer than during the first years of the present century. This church consists now of 288 members.

Edwards states in his history that " Mr. Wrightman, one of their ministers, was invited to preach at Fairfield in 1714, but forgetting his situation, he talked away as if he had been in a Baptist pulpit, and eight Presbyterians joined the society." But in a note he adds, " Since I have been informed but four joined Baptists, the other four were baptized to ease a scrupulous conscience, and then returned to their own church." Those were days of controversy. He says, " In 1742 a great stir in Cape May ; but some one of the party converts joining the other party, caused a howling among the losing shepherds and issued in a public challenge. Mr. Morgan accepted ; his antagonist was Rev. Mr. Finley. The contest ended as usual in a double triumph ; but two things happened to mar the glory of the day. One was a remark that a stander-by (Mr. Leeman) was heard to make. He was a deist, and therefore a disinterested person. He said, " The littleman (Finley) is thrown down, and his antagonist will not let him rise for another tussle." Both parties published their discourses.

Among the members of the old Fairfield congregation was Nathan Lawrence (or as he spelled his name, Lorrance), who was a large property owner at Cedarville, on the southern side of Cedar Creek. He became a Baptist, and was perhaps one of Wrightman's converts in 1714, and was so zealous in propagating his new faith as frequently to journey with the ministers to Cape May and other places. He erected a meeting-house on his own land, where the Baptist meeting-house now stands, a little south of the school-house. Dying early in 1745, he, by his will, dated November 23, 1744, left to his two sons, Jonathan and Nathan, and three daughters, several tracts of land and other property, and to his daughter Abigail Elmer (the writer's grandmother) "all that messuage called Flying Point, except one acre where the Baptist meeting-house now standeth, where the Baptist members that liveth on the south side of Cohansey Creek shall think fit to take it, to her or her heirs forever by her present husband, Daniel Elmer;" they to pay a certain sum to two of his daughters and complying with what shall be hereafter enjoined. "I also lay and enjoin a penalty on all or any of my afore-mentioned children, whereby they, any one or more, shall forfeit all their lands above mentioned, to their other brothers and sisters, to be equally divided between them, or pay ten pounds current money, amongst their brothers and sisters, for every time that any of them shall be convicted, or that it shall be made to appear by any one or more of them, that any one has agreed or obliged him or herself to pay, or has paid any sum of money, or any consideration whatsoever, toward supporting or maintaining minister or congregation of those called Presbyterians, direct or indirect."

This part of the will, however, appears to have been treated by all concerned as mere *brutem fulmen*, and disregarded. The daughter and husband were, or soon became, members of the Presbyterian church, and the other children supporters of it. The testator was buried in the ground annexed to the meeting-house, where his tombstone was formerly to be seen; but his two sons were buried in the old Cohansey graveyard, on the river side, at New England Town. The meeting-house does not appear to have been used by the Baptists, who were either ignorant of the will, or preferred to concentrate their support on the new house recently erected in lower Hopewell. During many years after this, those living south of the Cohansey were accustomed to cross that river at a place something more than a mile above Greenwich, which was long known as the Baptist Landing.

The house at Cedarville appears to have been possessed by Daniel Elmer during his life, and after the split in the Presbyterian church, it was said was frequently used by preachers of the new-light side, and among others, by the celebrated Whitfield, in 1748. It was removed by Timothy Elmer, son of Daniel, and converted into a barn on his property below the tavern of Cedarville, prior to 1780. The lot was afterwards, about 1828, sold under the Elmer title, although then claimed by the Baptists, who soon purchased it, and erected on it the house now in use.

A descendant of the Rev. Mr. Brooks, who states that he had been a member of the church thirty-two years, and a deacon twelve, had a bitter controversy in the year 1765 with Jonathan Bowen, father of Jonathan Bowen, afterwards of Bridgeton, who

was also a prominent member of the church, which involved in it
the pastor, Mr. Kelsey, whose daughter had married a son of Mr.
Bowen. This resulted in the expulsion of Mr. Brooks from the
church communion, and caused him to print, "A plowman's complaint against a clergyman, being a letter to the Baptist Association of Philadelphia." The pamphlet exhibits a sad want of temper, and shows that the prevalent habit of freely indulging in the
use of strong drink, which in those days occasioned much scandal
in all the churches, had much to do with it. . The dispute grew in
part out of a controversy about a lot claimed to belong to the parsonage, at the southwest corner of Bowentown Cross-roads. Mr.
Kelsey, it appears at length, preached a sermon, taking as his text
the 17th and 18th verses of the 16th chapter of Romans. This
was of course very offensive to the deacon, who proclaimed before
he left the house, and repeated it in his pamphlet, that he wished
the minister to preach Christ crucified, and not Jonathan Bowen
crucified.

Edwards says that in 1716 several of the Baptists embraced the
sentiments of the Sabbatarians, who insisted that the seventh day
Sabbath was of perpetual obligation. This led to the establishment of the Shiloh Seventh Day Baptist Church about the year
1736. The founders were John Sweeney, Dr. Elijah Bowen, John
Jarman, Rev. Jonathan Davis, Caleb Ayres, and others. About
the year 1790 a considerable number embraced the Universalist
sentiments of Winchester, some of whom became in fact deists,
whereby the society was much disturbed and troubled. This difficulty has now passed away, and the society, as well as the town
itself, surrounded by fertile land, has greatly improved. Their
tenets are believed to be the same as those of the regular Calvin-
istic Baptists, with the exception of that relating to the observance
of the Sabbath. At their first organization they erected a wooden
meeting-house, which, about the year 1761, was superseded by the
old brick building still standing on their burial-ground lot. This
latter was in its turn superseded in 1854 by the present neat edifice
of brick, a little nearer to the town than the old one. They have
also a neat and commodious school-house of two stories, in which
a good school is maintained.

An offset from this church has a building, not very distant, just
within the limits of Salem County.

A regular Baptist Church was formed at Dividing Creek, in

Downe Township, by members of the old Cohansey Church in the year 1761, and still continues to flourish, having now 222 members.

There were also for many years a church called the West Creek Baptist Church, a little west of the boundary between Cumberland and Cape May. The old meeting-house is still standing, but does not appear now to be used.

The Baptist church in Bridgeton, known as the Second Cohansey, was erected by the old Cohansey Church in 1816, during the pastorate of Mr. Smalley, and continued to worship in connection with them until 1828, when they were constituted a separate church, and the Rev. George Spratt was chosen their pastor. In 1857 they erected a new and larger building on the north side of Commerce Street. Their members now number 348.

Another offset from the old Cohansey is the church at Greenwich, which erected a neat edifice on the north side of the main street in 1844. They were constituted a separate church in 1850, and now number 115 members.

A church was constituted at Cedarville in 1836, and numbers now 114 members.

Millville Church was constituted in 1842, and has 44 members. That at Newport was constituted in 1852, and numbers 147 members. The aggregate number of members in all the regular Baptist churches of the county is 1218.

In 1863 a Baptist church was constituted in Vineland, and a meeting-house erected. In 1868 the old Second Cohansey Baptist meeting-house on Pearl Street, Bridgeton, was enlarged, and a new church constituted, which is now (1869) very flourishing.

No records or documents remain from which it can be ascertained when the "Cohansey Church" of Fairfield was first established, although there can be but little doubt that it was not later than 1690. At first it was like the churches of Connecticut, independent. The Presbytery of Philadelphia, with which it became united in 1708, was first established in 1705. Before this time a log meeting-house had been erected at the place known as New England Town Cross-Roads, probably on the lot situate on the south bank of the Cohansey, where the old graveyard still remains.

The first minister known to have preached here was the Rev. Thomas Bridges, belonging to a family of considerable importance in England, who graduated at Harvard College, and, after being engaged in mercantile pursuits, went to England, and returned to Boston in 1682, with testimonials from John Owen and other eminent Dissenters. He appears to have preached for some time in the West Indies. About the year 1695 he came to Cohansey, and located several tracts of land. How long he preached at Fairfield is uncertain; but he is said to have been called from there in 1702, to be the colleague of Mr. Bradstreet in Boston, where he died in 1715, at the age of fifty-eight. Whether any one succeeded Bridges before 1708 is unknown. Early in that year, at the instance of his college classmate, Jedediah Andrews, who came to Philadelphia in 1698, and became the pastor of the first Presbyterian church there, being ordained in 1701, Joseph Smith, a graduate of Harvard, who had been licensed as a preacher, came to Cohansey. Andrews wrote to him that they were "the best people of his neighborhood." Smith met the Presbytery in May, 1708, and was ordained and installed in May, 1709; but, complaining of negligence in making up his support, he soon returned to New England.

In 1710 Samuel Exell came to Cohansey, but in 1711 the Presbytery wrote to the people that, "by the best account they had of him, they judged him not a suitable person to preside in the work of the ministry." In 1712, John Ogden represented the church in the Presbytery as an elder, and by him a petition was sent to which no answer was returned. In 1713 Ephraim Sayre appeared as elder, and asked advice about the choice of a minister. They sent Howell Powell, who had been ordained in Wales, and he was installed pastor, continuing until 1717, when he died, leaving descendants still maintaining a respectable position in the county.

About this time, or perhaps sooner, the old log meeting-house was superseded by a comfortable frame building, covered on the sides, as well as the roof, with what in this country are called shingles. It stood on the southeast corner of the old graveyard, and was furnished only with benches, upon which the audience sat. About the year 1775 it became so dilapidated as to be unsafe to preach in, and the benches were taken out, and placed under a large white-oak tree at the corner of the lot, which has been cut down; and there, in good weather, the pastor preached. Old inhabitants of Fairfield have said, and probably with truth, that no person ever rode to this church in a wheeled vehicle. It was not until 1780 that the "old stone church," now in its turn deserted, was fit to preach in.

Henry Hook, from Ireland, came to Cohansey in 1718, and was installed pastor. During his time there was a congregation at Greenwich, to which it would seem that he ministered. In April, 1722, Andrews writing to Mather, says: "The week before last, by the pressing importunity of the minister of Cohansey, I went thither to heal some differences between the two congregations there, which being effected contrary to expectation, such charges were laid against him as have subverted him from acting there or anywhere else." He removed to Delaware, and the New Castle Presbytery met at Cohansey to investigate the case. The judgment was, that though several things were not proven, yet it was due to rebuke him openly in Fairfield meeting-house, and to suspend him for a season. Noyes Parris, a graduate of Harvard, preached to the congregation from 1724 to 1729, when having fallen under serious imputations, he in a disorderly manner withdrew to New England.

In 1729 Rev. Daniel Elmer came from Connecticut, and was ordained and installed the pastor. His wife, and the wife of Joseph Smith, who had been settled here a short time twenty years before, were connections of the Parsons family, so that it is probable Elmer was sent here by Smith. He was a graduate of Yale College, and had for some time taught a grammar school at West Springfield. He found the title of the property at New England Town in a very unsatisfactory situation. He, however, soon built himself a comfortable house, near the meeting-house, which was burned down shortly before his death. The church records were then destroyed. He cultivated the farm adjoining, and it is believed was sometimes employed as a surveyor, a business to which his eldest son Daniel was educated, and which he followed until his death.

In the year 1741 the great schism occurred in the Presbyterian body, by which it was separated into two parties, called old-lights and new-lights, Mr. Elmer adhering to the old-lights. Whitfield preached in 1740 at Greenwich, and produced a powerful effect on many of his hearers, including the younger Daniel Elmer, who was then married and lived at Cedarville. He joined the new side, and was accustomed, for several years, to pass by his father's meeting-house, and go to Greenwich, which had a new-light minister. When the meeting-house near his residence, built by his father-in-law Lorrance, came into his possession, he was in the habit of having the prominent new-lights preach there; and among them, the tradition always has been, Whitfield. This must have been during his second visit to this country, about 1747–8. It is certain that the breach went so far, that his children, born in 1750 and 1752, were baptized by Mr. Hunter, and not by his father, as the older ones had been. The writer heard from his father, that upon one occasion, when his son was present, the father preached on the subject of the schism, and became so pointed in his remarks that Daniel left the house. His father, seeing this movement, directed one of his elders to go out, and require him, in God's name, to return. He refused to obey the summons, and upon the elder being asked if he had summoned him in God's name, he replied, no; that he did not see that he had any authority to do that. Thereupon, after a considerable pause, the old gentleman said, "Perhaps we had better drop the subject," and did so. The minister appears to have frequently complained of his troubles to the Presbytery. In September, 1754, the Synod appointed a committee to endeavor to remove the difficulties in the congregation; but his death in January, 1755, put an end to the proceedings.*

* Rev. Daniel Elmer was the grandson of Edward Elmer, who came over from England to America as one of the congregation of Rev. Thomas Hooker, in 1632. They constituted a church at Cambridge, Massachusetts, but in 1636, with Hooker at their head, and carrying Mrs. H. in a litter, driving 160 cattle, for the sake of their milk to use by the way, and to stock a new settlement, went across the wilderness to Hartford, Connecticut. Edward was a magistrate, and purchased a large tract of land on the Podunk River, and was killed by the Indians in 1676.

The family name was originally Aylmer—in Latin, Almer—and were settled in England as early as 1306, one of them being a Chief Baron of the Exchequer. John Aylmer, who was educated at Oxford, and was a Protestant, was tutor of the celebrated and unfortunate Lady Jane Grey, and was, in 1568, by Queen Elizabeth, made Bishop of London, by the name of John Elmer. Edward is believed to have been his grandson.

Daniel Elmer had three sons and four daughters, all of whom left descendants, still remaining in the county, and now become very numerous. His oldest son, Daniel, born in Massachusetts, who died in 1761, clerk of the county court, was a leading citizen at Fairfield, and so was Theophilus. Most of the name now residing in Bridgeton are descendants of Daniel second, Charles E. Elmer, Esq., being the heir, according to the rules of the common law; and his son Daniel, the seventh oldest son in regular lineal descent, bearing that name.

Rev. Jonathan Elmer, long a prominent Presbyterian minister in Essex County, N. J., before the Revolution, was a cousin of Rev. Daniel, and has left descendants living in the northern part of the State and in New York. One of his brothers, who was a Colonel in the Connecticut line, was commissioned as Samuel Elmore,

The people now showed a disposition to unite, and in June, 1755, Thomas Ogden, one of the elders, proceeded to New Haven with a letter from Dr. Alison, of Philadelphia, to Mr. Stiles. He writes: "These wait on you in favor of the church at Fairfield, in New Jersey, which was formerly under the care of Mr. Daniel Elmer. They were divided in his time, but have now agreed, by advice of our Presbytery, to invite a minister from Connecticut, and, if they can be happily supplied, to bury all their contentions, and to unite under his ministry." No minister was found in Connecticut; but William Ramsey, of Irish descent, who had graduated at Princeton in 1754, soon went to Fairfield, and was licensed and ordained, and settled there by the Abingdon Presbytery, a new-light Presbytery, to which he belonged in 1756. In 1758 the breach of the Presbyterian church was healed, and the two hostile Synods united; after which Mr. Ramsey and his church joined the old Presbytery of Philadelphia. He was a man of ardent piety and eloquence, and succeeded in producing harmony. The members, as recorded in his record of the Session in 1759, were 78. In 1758 he married the eldest daughter of Col. Ephraim Seeley, of Bridgeton, his congregation including persons residing there and at the Indian fields. Col. Seeley was himself a Baptist, but his wife, in 1761, connected herself with Mr. Ramsey's church, and the family attended his services. Upon the occasion of his marriage his people purchased a parsonage, consisting of a farm of 150 acres in Sayres' Neck, about a mile southwest of where the old stone church now stands; and here he resided until his death in 1771. About 1765 a powerful revival of religious feeling occurred, in which, as recorded by Ebenezer Elmer, then about thirteen years old, "the young, in general, became very much engaged, and we had meeting at least twice a week during all the summer and fall." About sixty new members were added to the church.

He was succeeded by the Rev. William Hollinshead, who was quite distinguished as a preacher, and who was installed in 1773. The troubles and privations produced by the Revolutionary War

and having afterwards adopted that spelling, his descendants continue to write their names in that way. Several of the name of Elmore have lived in the Southern States, and perhaps still do; one of whom was formerly a senator of the United States from South Carolina, and one was Treasurer of the "Confederate States," when the seat of government was at Montgomery.

fell heavily on the congregation, and, to increase their difficulties, it became necessary to build a new meeting-house. The ground was purchased in 1775, and subscriptions obtained to commence the work. It was, however, suspended until 1780, when, under the energetic superintendence of Theophilus Elmer, one of the sons of Rev. Daniel Elmer, who resided at New England Town, it was resumed. In September, 1780, Mr. Hollinshead preached the first sermon in it, but a year elapsed before it was completed, and rules adopted for selling and renting the seats. Those down-stairs were rented at the annual rental of £65 10s., and those up-stairs at about £36; in all £100, or $266. In 1783 the society was incorporated by a special act of assembly; and in the same year Mr. Hollinshead left, having been chosen pastor of the principal church in Charleston, South Carolina, where he remained until his death. A very signal revival of religion occurred in the winter of 1780–81. The next spring forty-eight new members were added, and the succeeding winter forty-six more followed by a few others; in all, during these years, one hundred and fifteen.

In 1786 the parsonage was rented on shares. In 1788 the Rev. Ethan Osborn, then 30 years old, of Litchfield, Connecticut, having visited Philadelphia, was induced by the Rev. Dr. Sproat to extend his journey to Fairfield. He preached for them on trial, according to the fashion of the day, for six months. March 11th, 1789, the trustees' book records: "It was agreed to pay 15s. hard money per week for the keep of Mr. Osborn and horse." This sum was nominally two dollars; but paid in hard money, and making allowance for the difference in prices, was equivalent to five dollars in specie now. Having received a unanimous call to be pastor, he accepted it, and was ordained and installed December 3d, 1789.

In 1794 he married Elizabeth Riley, residing at Indian-fields near Bridgeton, whose parents formed a part of his congregation, and commenced housekeeping at the parsonage. After a few years, however, he preferred to follow the New England fashion of having a homestead of his own, and accordingly purchased, and enlarged the house, about a mile from his church, on the northeast side of the road to Cedarville, where he took up his residence in 1803, and continued to occupy it fifty-five years; transmitting it to his family, one of his sons now owning it. His salary at first was £100; soon after his marriage it was raised to £125, but in 1802 it was put back to the original sum. In 1803 it was fixed at $300 and of course included the use or rent of the parsonage farm. In 1807 it was resolved to sell the parsonage, and the salary was put at $400. In 1809 the salary was raised to $450, and in 1812 to $500. Upon this pittance he raised a large and interesting family, and although of course always straitened, lived, according to the habits of his day, in comfort. The writer well remembers calling at his house, with a company of young persons, to see his eldest daughter, then a young lady of prepossessing manners and appearance, in the year 1814. Some one asking for water, it was brought in a glass pitcher, but no drinking glasses. With a peculiar pleasant smile Mr. Osborn remarked, "I would tell you that all our glasses got broken, and in these war times we could not afford to buy any more, but it rather mortifies Mrs. Osborn (who was present), so I suppose I musn't say anything about it."

Mr. Osborn was a remarkable man, and obtained a character and influence, not only in his own congregation, but throughout the county, which no one else can expect to emulate. So scattered was his congregation, and such had been the effect of the destitution of preaching, following the removal of Mr. Hollinshead, that he found only 125 members on his arrival. But his labors were greatly blessed. In 1809 and 1810, there was a special awakening, so that 120 members were added to his church. In 1819 there was again a revival, 56 being added at one time. Again in 1827 there were 51 additions; and in 1831 about 80 were added. The total number of members at that time was 336; and the congregation had so increased that the old stone church had become filled. Not a pew, and scarcely a sitting either on the floor or in the spacious galleries, could be obtained by a new-comer. During his pastorate, which lasted fifty-five years, he admitted more than six hundred members to the communion of his church. In 1836, having reached his 78th year, Rev. David McKee was installed as co-pastor, and he relinquished $200 of his salary. Mr. McKee continued in this relation about two years. In 1844 Mr. Osborn resigned, at the age of 86. His last sermon was preached in 1850, in the old stone church, being a solemn farewell to that place, hallowed by so many endearing associations, and to the people so long under his charge. From this time his faculties gradually decayed; but he survived eight years longer; at the time of his decease, lacking only three months and twenty days to make his age one hundred years!

8

The lower part of the township having, during the fore part of this century, very considerably increased in population and wealth, a disposition began to be shown to establish a new church at Cedarville. In 1819 the question was brought to a vote of the congregation, when 43 voted in favor of the proposition and 45 against it. About 1837 occurred the division of the Presbyterian church into Old School and New School. Mr. Osborn belonged to the New School party, but the preference of many of his church was for the other side. This led to the establishment of the brick church at Cedarville, which now numbers 195 members.

A New School Presbyterian church was also established about the same time at Cedarville, which still continues, numbering 120 members. The congregation worshipping in the stone church soon removed to the village of Fairton, where a handsome edifice was erected, and the church there now numbers 140 members; claiming, it is believed without dispute, to be the legal successor of the old Cohansey Presbyterian Church; thus, after near a century and a half, multiplied to three; having three pastors and an aggregate of 355 members.

At what precise time a Presbyterian church was constituted at Greenwich there is no means of knowing. From the letter of Andrews, referred to in the account of the church at Fairfield, it appears there was a separate congregation there before 1722, to whom the minister at Fairfield was accustomed to preach. There was a constant intercourse between the two places, many of the settlers at Greenwich having gone there from Fairfield. Both places, although spoken of for many years as Cohansey, or as in Cohansey, were named from towns in Connecticut. In 1717 land was conveyed by Jeremiah Bacon to trustees, for the people called Presbyterian on the north side of Cohansey. Although this mode of referring to them has been thought to indicate that they were constituted a distinct church before this time, the language is entirely consistent with the people being still connected with the Cohansey church at Fairfield. Settlers were constantly arriving from Scotland and the north of Ireland, most of whom established themselves on the north side of Cohansey, so that while the New England element prevailed at Fairfield it was otherwise at Greenwich; and when the division occurred, the former, as a general rule, adhered to the old side, while the latter were warm supporters of the New Lights, or followers of Whitfield.

There is no evidence in the minutes of the Presbytery and Synod of an organized church at Greenwich until 1728, when Ebenezer Gould, a graduate of Yale, and friend of Daniel Elmer, was installed the pastor. A wooden meeting-house was erected a little before this time, but in a few years was superseded by one of brick 34 by 44 feet, which was not finished until 1751, although occupied for worship several years sooner. It was considered at this time the largest and most imposing church edifice in South Jersey. At first the only pews it contained were those constructed around the walls, each pew being built at the expense of its occupant, the area in the middle being furnished with benches. The galleries were originally reached by a stairway on the outside of the building. It stood on the lot still used as a burial place at the place usually called the "head of Greenwich," and remained until —— when one of brick was erected on the opposite side of the street; enlarged to its present dimensions in 1860.

Gould left in 1739 and went to Long Island. The church remained vacant several years, but was from time to time supplied by Tennant, Blair, and other eminent ministers of the new-side. The celebrated Whitfield preached here in 1740, not in the church building, which could not hold his hearers, but on the side of the hill, northeast of the church, then covered with the original forest. His journal records that he crossed the Delaware from Philadelphia in the morning of Monday, preached in the middle of the day at Gloucester, then the county seat, and in the evening at Greenwich, where he passed the night. This was at or near the place now called Clarksboro', then and still the township of Greenwich. On the next day he rode to Pilesgrove, now Pittsgrove, and preached there. The next day he preached at what he calls Cohansey, no doubt meaning Greenwich, from whence on the next day he went to Salem and preached there. At Greenwich, his journal states, "The words gradually struck the hearers till the whole congregation was greatly moved, and two cried out in the bitterness of their souls after a crucified Saviour, and were scarcely able to stand."

Andrew Hunter, from Ireland, an uncle of another Andrew Hunter, father of the present General Hunter, and of Andrew Hunter, Esq., deceased, an eminent lawyer at Trenton, and formerly Attorney-General of this State, was settled in 1746 by the New Brunswick Presbytery, controlled by the New Lights with which the church remained connected until the union of the two parties, when it returned to the Presbytery of Philadelphia. He was also installed pastor of the Deerfield church, this connection remaining until 1760. He died in 1775 of a malignant dysentery, which was very fatal that year. A vacancy then occurred, during the troublesome time of the Revolution, and the church was obliged to depend upon casual supplies. In 1782 George Faitoute was installed, remaining until 1790, when he removed to Long Island. He, however, occasionally officiated afterwards at Greenwich, the writer having been baptized by him there in 1793.

In 1795 a union was formed with the newly-constituted church at Bridgeton, and William Clarkson was installed as the joint-pastor, remaining until 1801, when he removed to Savannah. Jonathan Freeman succeeded him in 1805, and remained pastor until 1822, when he died. The practice of these ministers was to preach in the morning of the Sabbath at Greenwich, and in the afternoon at Bridgeton. After 1810, when Mr. Freeman took up his residence in Bridgeton, he also preached in the court-house in the evenings of Sunday and Wednesday.

A parsonage farm was purchased for the Greenwich pastor in 1754, near Bowentown, immediately south of the Baptist parsonage. Mr. Clarkson and Mr. Freeman both resided here during the early part of their settlement, but they both soon removed to Bridgetown. It was sold in 1811.

The upper part of Deerfield and Hopewell townships, especially in the neighborhood of the streams flowing into the Cohansey, having a fertile soil, were settled at a pretty early date, among whom were a number of Presbyterians. They, in union with the people of Pilesgrove, of which Pittsgrove then made a part, took measures as early as 1732 to organize a religious society. In 1737 a log building was erected for worship in Deerfield, and the Rev. Daniel Buckingham preached there, and at Pilesgrove, in 1738. The Pilesgrove people insisted upon having a distinct organization, and after much contention, a commission of the presbytery acceded to their request, on condition that the house should not be nearer to the Deerfield house than six miles. David Evans was settled at Pilesgrove, but the Deerfield Church went over to the new side, and depended on supplies until they united with Greenwich, in 1746, and Mr. Hunter became the pastor of the united churches. This connection, being found too inconvenient, was dissolved in 1760.

The next pastor at Deerfield was Simon Williams, who was settled in 1764, and remained two years. In 1767 Enoch Green became the pastor, and so continued until 1776, when he died. He was much esteemed as a preacher and scholar. For several years he taught a classical school. In 1777 John Brainerd, a brother of the celebrated missionary, David Brainerd, was settled. He died in 1781. Both these ministers were buried there. In 1783 Simon Hyde was installed, but he died during the same year. In 1786 William Pickles, an Englishman of extraordinary eloquence, was installed. It was not long, however, before he showed himself unfit for the office, and he was deposed by the Presbytery. John Davenport succeeded him, being installed in 1795, and was dismissed in 1805. Nathaniel Reeve was installed in 1795, removing in 1817 to Long Island. Several others have succeeded, in all not less than seven. The church is now prosperous, numbering 145 members. This church is believed to be the only one in the county retaining a farm attached to the parsonage. Besides the farm it owns a considerable tract of wood land, which has been the means, by the sale of the wood, of adding considerably to its resources. The stone church now occupied was built in 1771 and enlarged and improved in 1859.

Bridgeton remained without any organized church, or any place of worship but the court-house, forty-five years after it became the county town. The Presbyterians residing there or in the vicinity worshipped at Fairfield or Greenwich, and the Baptists at the old Cohansey church, in Lower Hopewell. The question of having a church in the town began to be agitated, however, about 1770. An unexecuted will of Alexander Moore, on file in the surrogate's office, dated in that year, contains a devise of a lot of land 13 by 15 perches, lying within and described on the plan of the town made for him by Daniel Elmer, on the east side of the river, for the sole use of a Presbyterian meeting-house and burial-ground; and also a legacy of £50, to aid in building the house. The lot was situated on the north side of Commerce Street, a little above where Pearl Street now is. In 1774 some subscriptions were made to carry out this plan, and stone was brought on the lot, but the building was never commenced. The stones were used in building a house, which used to stand nearly opposite the proposed site at the corner of Commerce and Pearl Streets, which for many years was owned and occupied by Mark Riley, who belonged to a family from Connecticut who settled at an early day on the Indian Field tract.

At this time, and during several years afterwards, the most influential, and indeed the larger part of the inhabitants, lived on the west side of the river. There was no little strife in regard to the site. Dr. John Fithian offered a lot at the southeast corner of Broad and Giles Streets. Several meetings, to agree upon the place, were held without any result. At length, in 1791, through the influence of Dr. Jonathan Elmer, Col. Potter and Gen. Giles, Mark Miller, the son and heir of Ebenezer Miller, who was a Friend, agreed in consideration of a promise made by his father, to give the lot, containing two acres, then and still at the extreme west end of the town, "to be used, occupied, and enjoyed by the inhabitants of Bridgetown forever, for the purposes of a burying-ground for all said inhabitants generally, and for erecting thereon a house for the public worship of Almighty God." To this lot additions were made by subsequent purchases.

About £600, or $1600, were subscribed, and the building commenced in 1792, but the money raised was only sufficient to put up the walls and roof of the house. In 1793 a law of the State was obtained, authorizing the trustees to raise $2000 by means of a lottery, in accordance with a practice then very common. By this means the money was obtained, and in 1795 the house was so far completed as to be opened for public worship. At this time the public, or, as it was still called by old people, the King's highway to Greenwich, ran through the middle of the lot, a little south of the church building; but it was now altered by extending to Broad Street, or, as it was then called, High or Main Street, up to Fourth Street, as West Street was then called, and the road to Greenwich passed to the north and west of the church lots. The fence around the graveyard was first put up and the old King's highway closed in 1802. Many of the posts, which were of red cedar, are now, after a lapse of sixty years, in good condition. In 1792 a church had been duly constituted by the Presbytery of Philadelphia, which united with the church at Greenwich, and so continued until the death of Mr. Freeman in 1822.

Brogan Hoff became the pastor in 1824, and left in 1833. The session-house at the corner of Commerce and Pearl Streets was built in 1826, and continued to be used there for lectures, prayer meetings, and the Sabbath school until 1863, when it was removed to its present site.   In 1834 John Kennedy became the pastor, and removed in 1838.

In 1835 the congregation resolved to build a new church edifice on the east side of the river, which was done, and the house on Laurel Street was opened for worship in 1836.   In 1839 Samuel B. Jones became the pastor, and continued until 1863, when he resigned.   It contains now 281 members.

A second Presbyterian church was organized in 1838, and the stone church on Pearl Street erected in 1840, at first in connection with the New School Presbytery of Philadelphia, but afterwards united with the Presbytery of West Jersey.   It has 120 members. Recently, in 1869, a new building has been commenced on Commerce Street, and a church organized called the West Presbyterian Church of Bridgeton.

A Presbyterian church was organized at Port Elizabeth in 1820, but was soon removed to Millville, where most of the elders and members resided.   In 1838 a house was erected in the latter place which was enlarged in 1855.   There are now 73 members.   There is also a new church at Vineland.   The whole number of Presbyterian churches in the county at this time being nine, three of which are in connection with the New School Presbytery, and six with the West Jersey Presbytery, Old School, numbering together about 1250 members.

Smith, in his History of New Jersey, published in 1765, describing the then condition of Cumberland, states that the places of worship were Episcopalians one, Presbyterian four, Baptist two, Seventh-day Baptist one, Quakers one.   What place of worship of Presbyterians besides those at Fairfield, Greenwich, and Deerfield, he refers to, is uncertain.   Probably it was a church erected by the German settlers in Upper Hopewell, near the place now called New Boston, about the year 1760, which it appears by the deed was called the German Presbyterian Church.   It is not known whether it ever had a regular pastor, the building never having been finished.   It stood, however, until about the year 1812, and the graveyard still remains.   The worshippers united with the neighboring Presbyterian churches.   The Swedes erected a church on the east side of Maurice River, opposite Buckshootem, in 1743, in which worship was maintained by the Missionaries from Sweden, until after the Revolutionary War, when it went to decay, and has long since entirely disappeared.

An Episcopal church was erected at Greenwich about the year 1729, by Nicholas and Leonard Gibbon, of the established church in England, on land belonging to the last named. It is not known whether it was ever regularly consecrated and received as a regular church edifice, although it was occasionally used for service by the rector of the Salem church. After the removal and death of the founders, it seems to have fallen into neglect. The building, which was of brick, or a part of it, was for some years occupied as a stable, and some thirty years ago was entirely taken down. Leonard Gibbon and his wife were buried in the chancel. Recently their remains were carefully removed by some of their descendants and deposited in the Presbyterian graveyard. It was found upon this occasion, although the gravestones were in the proper positions, that, either by mistake or design, the husband had been buried at the side of his wife, with his head in the direction of her feet.

A church of the Episcopal order was established in Bridgeton in 1860, which has erected a handsome edifice on Commerce Street, and settled a rector, having —— members. There are also Episcopal churches in Millville and Vineland, in which there are regular services by a missionary.

There are also Roman Catholic chapels in Millville, Port Elizabeth, and in Bridgeton.

The German population of Bridgeton to the number of about 100, in conjunction with others in Millville, maintain a Lutheran minister, who preaches at the two places on alternate Sundays in the German language. A new church building has been commenced on York Street, Bridgeton. There is also a neatly erected chapel in Upper Deerfield, in connection with the Lutheran church that has long existed at Friesburg, in which the preaching is now in the English language.

Mark Reeve and others at Greenwich applied, in 1690, to the Salem monthly meeting of Friends, to assist them in building a meeting-house, which was erected where the present old Friends' meeting-house now stands, on a part of Reeve's sixteen acre lot. It was what is termed an indulged meeting, or meeting for worship only, being under the care of Salem meeting, and continued so until 1770, when this and the meeting at Alloway's Creek were united and formed one monthly meeting, to be held alternately at each place. The number of Friends that settled at Greenwich or elsewhere in the county was never large. At the time of the great division of the society in 1836, into the two parties generally called Orthodox and Hicksite, the former being the most considerable in number, retained the old building where they still worship. The members of both sexes number about ——. The other party built a new house on the main street about a mile northward of the old one, and continue to worship there. They number about —— members.

A Friends' meeting-house still remains at Port Elizabeth, built in 1800, but the society is now nearly or quite extinct.

The first Sunday school taught in the county was opened in the Academy on Bank Street, Bridgeton, by Ebenezer Elmer, in 1816. In the course of a few months a regular society was formed and a school commenced in the old court-house, which continued to be taught there until 1829, when it was removed to the new session-house at the corner of Commerce and Pearl Streets. While kept in the court-house although most of the teachers and scholars were Presbyterians, it was a union school. At first, owing to a strange misconception of the true object of such schools, which is to teach religious truths and other learning, only as a means of acquiring religious knowledge, many even religious and well-informed persons opposed them. Some thought they would interfere with that family and pastoral instruction of youth which Presbyterians especially had always practised, while others held back from that reluctance to understand and engage in a new enterprise which is so common. At first these schools were looked to mainly as a means of instruction for the poor. Soon, however, the great good found uniformly to result from their establishment, not only to the poor and neglected classes but to all the youth, recommended them so strongly that they were gradually introduced at different places. About 1830 they were adopted by the churches of all denominations, lost their union character, and are now carried on in connection with most of the places of religious worship in the county by the different societies using them.

The Methodists made but little progress in the United States until after the Revolution. Almost all the preachers were from Great Britain, and all imitated John Wesley in their hostility to the resistance made by the colonies to the measures adopted by the King and Parliament. It was not until 1784 that they became an independent society, and adopted the name of the Methodist Episcopal Church of the United States. Prior to this time the sacraments and other ordinances were administered only by the bishops and priests of the Episcopal church, or in rare instances by the ministers of other denominations, to which the converts to Methodism happened to be attached. The first annual conference, which was held in 1773, appointed John King and William Watters to travel and preach in Jersey. Watters is said to have been the first native American appointed as a travelling preacher. The salary allowed in 1784 was sixty-four dollars, and the same sum to the wife if there was one. The preachers, however, were entertained without charge to them by their converts and other friends, who commonly had some allowance made to them for doing so by the societies.

As early as the year 1780 there were some converts to Methodism at Port Elizabeth and its vicinity. The first church building in the county for the exclusive use of this society was erected there in 1786, on ground donated for the purpose by Mrs. Bodley. A Mr. Donnelly, who was a local preacher there, died before this time. In 1798 Dr. Benjamin Fisler, who commenced his ministry in 1791 and preached in Camden, and in 1797 travelled on the Salem Circuit with William McLenahan, which included Salem, Cumberland, Cape May, and a considerable part of Gloucester County, on account of his feeble health, located at Port Elizabeth, where he was an acceptable local preacher for half a century. He was an intelligent man, who had read a good deal, and although a firm believer in the doctrines taught by Benson and Watson, had no respect for Dr. Clarke's Commentary, which he thought contained many dangerous errors. He once told the writer he would not allow Clarke's Life of the Wesley Family, interesting as it is, to be read by his children, on account of the currency it gives to the story of the ghost, thought to have haunted the house of John Wesley's father, which practised rappings something like those made by the modern spiritualists. In those days ghosts were received with more credit than now ; Wesley's belief in them having influenced many of his followers.

About the same time Eli Budd, from Burlington County, belonging to a family of Friends, who were among the original settlers of that county, several of whom became Methodists, and some were preachers, purchased land on the upper part of Manamuskin, and commenced making iron. His son Wesley was quite distinguished as a preacher, and in 1799 rode the Salem Circuit. Afterwards he established iron-works at the place long called Cumberland Furnace, now Manamuskin Manor; but in the language of Raybold, whose "Reminiscences of Methodism in West Jersey," contains many interesting particulars of which free use has been made, "he made a shipwreck of his character, happiness and hope," and it may be added that he also made shipwreck of his worldly prosperity, having failed in 1818, and being unable to retrieve his fortune, soon left the State. His father and brother maintained a good character. Early in this century a church was built near the iron-works and a society organized, which, however, when the works were abandoned in —— soon became nearly or quite extinct. Recently it has been revived. Fithian Stratton, a famous but very eccentric preacher, also gathered a society at his settlement on Menantico. He was originally a member of the Presbyterian church in Deerfield, and fell under church censure for improper conduct apparently growing out of his violent temper in 1779, and appears to have afterwards abandoned that church and joined himself to the Methodists. Preachers of this denomination began to gather societies within the bounds of the Deerfield congregation as early as 1780, in which and in subsequent years some members of that church were censured for irregularly withdrawing from its communion and joining the Methodists without a regular dismission. In 1799, Mr. Stratton, who had then become a Methodist preacher, sent a written request to the pastor and session to be permitted to preach in the church; but this was denied on the ground of his previous conduct. He died in 1811, soon after which his projected borough at Schooner Landing came to an end.

The church now called Woodruffs, in the neighborhood of Carllsburg, was composed originally of several Presbyterians from the Deerfield church. The meetings were held at first in a schoolhouse; Preston Stratton, the class-leader, being a brother of Fithian. In its best days this class had about twenty members. When Preston Stratton left, his place was supplied by Joel Harris, but he also soon moved away, and the class went down, the members joining another class in Broad Neck. Preaching was resumed in 1823 and a new class established in 1824, of which the late Judge Woodruff became the leader. In 1829 a house was built to be used as a school-house as well as for preaching, and after this there was regular preaching. In 1841 the existing church building was erected, the membership then being twenty-five. This church has never been a principal station, but has been either a part of a circuit, or of some other station, sometimes Bridgeton, sometimes Willow Grove, sometimes Pittsgrove in Salem County, and now of Cohansey.

Port Elizabeth circuit has connected with it five other churches one of which, viz., West Creek, where there were Methodists as early as 1790, and a church edifice was built in 1826, is in Cape May. Some of the members, however, reside in this county. At Heislerville the gospel was preached first in a private house in 1800. A meeting-house was erected in 1828, superseded in 1852 by a new and larger edifice. Leesburg society was commenced, about 1806, and the old church built about 1816, taken down in 1864, and a new and handsome building substituted. It is called "Hickman Church." Dorchester is a branch from Leesburg, formed in 1856, and a house built the same year. The old church, which was at one time the place of worship of a flourishing society while Cumberland furnace was carried on, but which had become dilapidated and the society almost extinct, had its place supplied by a new edifice in 1862, and the prospect now is that its congregation will steadily increase.

Michael Swing was the pioneer of the Methodists in Fairfield, to which place he came from Pennsylvania about the year 1790. He began, according to the usual practice, to hold meetings in private houses, and being a man of property and the owner of a farm adjoining the old Presbyterian graveyard on Cohansey Creek, which in his lifetime belonged to the Rev. Daniel Elmer, he in 1719, very much at his own expense, built the church near New Englandtown Cross-roads, which has ever since been known as the Swing meeting-house. It was for a long time the only Methodist meeting-house in the township, and was the third or fourth in the county.

Raybold tells us that in 1800, R. Swain and R. Lyon travelled the Salem Circuit, and that on one occasion Lyon announced at a meeting held in Fairfield, that on that day four weeks he would be there, "preach, pray, work a miracle, and have a revival." Swing (Irving he calls him) disapproved this proceeding, and wrote to Swain to try and meet Lyon at Fairfield, in order to keep him in order. Both the preachers attended at the appointed time, and there was a great crowd, excited by the announcement of the miracle. Swain preached; then Lyon arose and proclaimed, "Lyon is here, and he will yet preach; the miracle is there," pointing with his hand; "whoever saw the Presbyterian minister and his flock here before? Now, I shall preach, and the Lord will do the rest; we shall see the revival." He did preach, and a great revival followed, and the whole affair passed from the minds of the people, who were too happy in grace to be very critical. This proceeding, strange as it now seems, was very much in character with many things done by the early preachers, and the part assigned to Mr. Swing agrees with his character. He was a prudent man, an excellent preacher, and much esteemed not only by his own society, but by pious people of other denominations. He was a zealous and active member, and officer of the Cumberland Bible Society until his death in 1834, at a time when most of the Methodists declined to unite with it.

The church he built is now a separate station; called from the name of the town near by, Fairton. Formerly it belonged to Cumberland circuit, and was then made a station in connection with Cedarville, where a society was formed in 1833 and a church edifice erected in 1836. Cedarville became a separate station in 1861.

Methodist circuit riders, local preachers, and exhorters appear to have established meetings in many different parts of the county between 1780 and 1800. The whole county, and most of the time Cape May, belonged to the Salem circuit until about 1809, and the district of New Jersey included the whole State and a considerable part of New York. In 1811 the district was divided into two, but was united in 1816 and so remained until separated in 1823. In 1847 the upper part of the State became a part of Newark Conference, the lower part, south of Elizabeth, being the New Jersey Conference, comprising four districts, with each a presiding elder.

The labors of the itinerant preachers were very arduous and self-denying, and were greatly blessed in the conversion of many sinners. Raybold gives this illustration of what he terms a cure for the itinerant fever, as related to him by one of the circuit riders: "Many years ago I travelled Cumberland circuit. There was residing upon the circuit a brother P——, a most devotedly pious young man, and a local preacher of some few years' standing. He resided upon a good farm of his own, where with his small family he could live very comfortably indeed, and make money too; but whenever I went there he could talk of little else than travelling to preach the gospel more fully. He was of rather a

feeble frame and delicate health, and I informed him, it was my
judgment he never could stand constant labor in preaching, while
he could make himself very useful in his present position. The
Lord, I told him, did not require of men a work for which they
were physically unfitted. All my reasoning would not satisfy him;
so at last, during the winter, I requested him to meet me at a certain point and take a tour of two weeks on his native circuit, and
after that he could tell, perhaps, whether travelling and preaching
agreed with his constitution. At the appointed time and place we
met. For a week the appointments required two sermons a day;
and on Sundays three sermons, besides meeting classes and other
business matters; travelling for many miles through the woods
and over bad roads on horseback, in weather severely cold, for a
greater part of the time. I kept him at work steadily, occasionally
meeting the class myself. Towards the end of the second week, I
found he was becoming too feeble to go on much farther.

"One morning, as we started for the next daily task, heavy clouds
hung over, the wind howled among the trees, and snow began
to fall quite thickly. Brother P—— stopped his horse, and said,
'Had we not better put up somewhere? it will be a storm.' 'A storm,'
I replied; 'we never stop for a small snow-storm.' Poor P——
wrapped himself closer in his overcoat, and said no more. That
night finished the work of the circuit for the time; we had finished
the two weeks, and he was anxious to start for home, distant some
forty miles. The family where we stayed were up at three o'clock
to start for market, and brother P—— entreated me to arise at
breakfast and start for home. To please him I did so. We were
soon on the saddle, and in the clear moonlight of an intensely cold
morning we rode about twenty miles without a word of conversa-
tion. As the sun arose we came in sight of my residence, but he
had to travel twenty miles farther to reach his home. When we
were about to part, he stopped his horse, and I said, 'Now, P——,
what do you think of the itinerancy?' 'Ah, brother,' said he, 'it will
not do for me; I cannot stand it; I had no idea of the toil and ex-
posure, the privations and sufferings.' 'Why, my dear brother,' said
I, 'you have been on the lightest work, and in the best part of the
circuit; if this specimen discourages you, I do not know what you
would say to other scenes.' 'Ah,' said he, 'I had better stay at home
and attend to my family and farm, and leave the itinerancy to
those who are stronger than I am; this trial will satisfy me.' Poor

P—— went home, and had a spell of sickness, but he was cured of the travelling fever."

Bridgeton was for several years within the Salem circuit. John Walker, one of the preachers, formed a class about the year 1804, several Methodists having before this moved into the place. William Brooks, who then carried on a tannery at the southeast corner of Broad and Atlantic Streets, on the west side of the river, was the class-leader, and his house was usually the place of meeting and of entertainment for the preachers. Among the early converts was Jonathan Brooks, who was for many years a local preacher, and the leading Methodist of the town.

He was a good specimen of an old-fashioned Methodist. An illiterate man, knowing very little but what he learned from the Bible, and his own experience as a Christian, of good practical sense in all matters not too much influenced by his prejudices, an earnest exhorter, and maintaining a character above suspicion, he exercised a great and deserved influence, not only in his own society, but among the Christian people of other denominations. He had no toleration, however, for any departure from the early usages of the society; thought a minister would be spoiled by rubbing his back against a college, and opposed till the last, singing in church by note, or with the aid of a choir. Having been himself ordained as a deacon, and not entitled to administer the sacraments, he considered himself deprived of a privilege he ought to have, and was earnest for a reform, which he did not live to see. When the first Conference, at which Bishop Hedding presided, was held in Bridgeton in 1838, he groaned not only in spirit, but very audibly, that only one minister appeared with the old Wesley coat, and but very few exhibited any other than white pocket handkerchiefs, remarking to the writer, that the passion for an educated ministry, singing out of music-books., &c, with which all the young people were so taken, he feared would ruin the church.

The building now used as a chapel, and standing at the corner of Bank and Washington Streets, was erected where the brick church now stands on Commerce Street, in 1807, and was consecrated by Rev. Joseph Totten, then the presiding elder of the district, whose residence was on Staten Island. Before long Cumberland Circuit was established, of which this church formed a part until 1832, when it became a separate station, and so remains. The new brick church was built in 1833. It deserves notice as showing the importance of the two towns; that now the district covering the southern counties of the State is called Bridgeton district, and Salem ranks as a station. The brick church on Fayette Street, called Trinity, was erected in 1854, and that on Bank Street, called the Central M. E. Church, in 1866. Nothing perhaps marks more decidedly the change in the Methodist church than that nearly all the circuits of the county have been abolished, and now most of the principal churches have separate pastors.

Millville contained a few Methodists as early as 1810. Long before this time a class existed at White Marsh, distant about four miles, between Millville and Fairfield. The meetings for preaching in the town were for some time held in a building erected as a school and meeting-house for all denominations. In 1817 it was a regular station of the circuit riders, and about the year 1822 a building of stone, commenced for a dwelling, was purchased and converted into a church. In 1844 the old church was taken down and the edifice, now called the First Church, erected in its place. In 1857, the Second Church, in the upper part of the town, near the cotton mills, was erected.

There were a considerable number of Methodists within the boundaries of the township of Downe as early as 1800, in which year a class was formed at Haleysville, a settlement a little west of Mauricetown. In 1811 a church building was erected there, which was occupied until 1864, when it was superseded by a new one. In Mauricetown the society worshipped in a school-house until 1842, when a church was erected, and this church now gives the name to the station. A Captain Webb, of the English navy, is said to have landed at Nantuxet before 1800, and preached a sermon in a barn, and thus commenced a Methodist society, who built a meeting-house in 1804, which was burned in 1812. The society after this used a store house. In —— they erected the present building at Newport.

A society was commenced at Dividing Creek in the early part of this century, who erected a house in ——.

There is also a mission station at Port Norris, one at Buckshutem, and another at Centregrove.

A class of Methodists was formed and met in the school-house at Jericho, some time before 1842, and in 1846 they erected the meeting-house in which they now worship at Roadstown. In 1856 the house in Upper Hopewell, called Harmony, was erected. These two churches are now united in one station.

Full statistics of the numbers during the successive years that have elapsed since its commencement, if they could be obtained, would present us a proof of the peculiar adaptedness of this society to expand and fill up the waste places in the land, and of the remarkable and praiseworthy zeal and energy of the preachers and members. The number of members returned for Salem circuit in 1789 was 680, and in 1790 it was increased to 933. In 1808 the Cumberland circuit, which then included Cape May, returned 700 members. In 1832 Bridgeton station returned 357 members, one preacher, and Cumberland circuit 955 members and two preachers; returned, being only those belonging to the Conference, and not including the local preachers and exhorters, of which there were several. The Minutes of the Conference for 1864 returns Bridgeton, Commerce Street, 542 members; Trinity, 220; Roadstown and Harmony, 98; Fairton, 133; Cedarville, 145; Newport, 160; Mauricetown, 273; Millville (Second Street), 460; Millville (Foundry) 175; Vineland, 35; Port Elizabeth, 504; Woodruff and Cohansey, 86; numbering in all 2831 members, besides those returned as probationers. Some of the members returned as belonging to the Port Elizabeth Station, reside in the county of Cape May, but there are others connected with stations out of the bounds of the county who reside within it, so that the number in the county may be safely set down at 2800. Making all due allowance for the greater facility of becoming members of this society as compared with some other denominations, this certainly exhibits a wonderful progress. And when it is added, that the society has constantly employed about ten regular ministers besides twelve or more local preachers, and that the gospel is statedly preached nearly every Sunday and frequently on other days in at least twenty different houses, the evidence of zeal and industry is very complete.

Besides the white congregations, there are two places of worship occupied by the colored persons, one at Springtown and one at Piercetown, who are supplied by circuit riders appointed by a colored presiding elder, there being, by a late arrangement, two distinct districts of colored preachers who belong to the General Conference of the Methodist Episcopal Church. These two societies have about 80 members.

The Methodist Protestant church originated about the year 1828.

Soon after they built a meeting-house at Cedarville, which, however, after a few years, was sold, and belongs now to the New School Presbyterians. In 1847 a society was organized in the old school-house called "Friendship," on the road leading to Centreville; subsequently a new building was put up there and it is now connected with Bridgeton, where a house was erected on Laurel Street in 1861. The members of the two number about 160. There are also small societies and places for preaching at Newport, Port Norris, Millville and Cassaboom, a few miles northeast of that place. There are about 120 members in these societies, making the whole number about 280 members.

The first African Methodist Episcopal church in this county was formed at Springtown in 1817, and the members then and for some time afterwards were commonly called Allenites, from the name of their first bishop, who resided in Philadelphia. Their first small church was burned and was replaced in 1838 by the present edifice of stone. This society has now 126 members.

At Gouldtown a society was formed in 1820, and after a few years the school-house in which they worshipped until recently, which was built originally by Presbyterians at a place about a mile and a half northeast of its present location, was presented to them and moved. The existing neat edifice was built in 1861; the number of members is 85.

A society was formed at Port Elizabeth in 1836, a meeting-house built in 1838, and there are now 19 members. The society in Backneck, Fairfield Township, was formed in 1838, built a house in 1850, and has now 12 members.

The Bridgeton society was formed in 1854, and the next year erected their meeting house in the southwestern part of the town. There are now 92 members, of which about 27 have been added recently. A society was formed at Millville in 1864, which is taking measures to erect a house, numbering now 16 members. It will be thus seen that the colored race, depressed as they are by many discouraging circumstances, have the gospel preached to them, and have about as many church members in proportion to their numbers, as the more fortunate whites.

CHAPTER VI.

CURRENCY OF NEW JERSEY.

THE character and amount of the money circulating in a community is always an important element in determining its true condition. It is, however, exceedingly difficult to ascertain what were the facts of the case a few centuries back in any part of the civilized world, and this difficulty is not diminished, but is greatly increased, when we inquire into the situation of a new settled country. None of the historians of the American colonies seem to have given much attention to this subject, so that they afford us but little information in regard to it. All accounts, however, agree in showing that money was very scarce during the first century after their settlement. The money of account, as soon as the Dutch government was relinquished, was universally the same as that in England, namely, pounds, shillings, and pence. A limited amount of English coin, brought over by the immigrants, and a few Spanish and Portuguese gold coins were in circulation, but the most common coins were the "pieces of eight," as the Spanish milled dollars were called, and their subdivisions into halves, quarters, and eighths. It appears by some proceedings of the Assembly of Pennsylvania that pewter and lead coins were used for small change in 1698, and there is some reason to believe that a small leaden coin was used at a somewhat earlier period in New York. Gold and silver coins cut into parts were resorted to, and were a source of much inconvenience and loss up to the period of the Revolution, and since.

All the coins in use, it would seem, passed in the colonies at a higher rate than their actual value in England and elsewhere. They would naturally pass for something above the rate of foreign exchange which varied at different places and times. But legislators in those days, as well as some now, supposed that the value of coins or other money might be arbitrarily established by law. The Assembly of West Jersey, by an act passed in 1681, declared that old England money should advance in country pay, viz: The shilling to eighteen pence, and other English coins proportionably, and a New England shilling to fourteen pence, but they declared the next year that this act should be null and void. In 1693 the same Assembly, after reciting that it had been found very inconvenient that money in the province hath differed in value from the same coin current of our neighboring province of Pennsylvania, to prevent which inconveniency for the future, it was enacted that all pillar Mexico and "Sivil" pieces of eight, of twelve pennyweight, should pass current for six shillings; thirteen pennyweights, six shillings and two pence, and so on, advancing in nearly the same proportion up to seventeen pennyweights for seven shillings, smaller pieces in proportion; all "dog dollars"* at six shillings. In 1686 the Assembly of East Jersey passed an act establishing the value of a piece of eight, weighing fourteen pennyweights, at six shillings, and other coins in that proportion, but it was repealed in less than a year. The two governments were surrendered to the crown in 1702, and the value of money, so far as a law could regulate it, was established by Queen Anne's proclamation. There is reason to believe that in 1700, or within a few years after that date, the ordinary rate of the piece of eight, weighing not less than seventeen pennyweights, was in Boston six shillings, in New York eight shillings, in New Jersey and Pennsylvania seven shillings sixpence, and in Maryland four shillings sixpence.

This variance was much complained of by the English merchants, so that in 1704 Queen Anne issued a proclamation for settling and ascertaining the currency rates of foreign coins in the American plantations. After reciting the inconveniences occasioned by the different rates of the coin, and that the officers of the mint had laid before her a table of the value of the several foreign coins which actually pass in payment in the plantations, according to the weight and assays thereof, viz., Seville pieces of eight, old plate, seventeen pennyweights, twelve grains, four shillings and sixpence; Mexican and pillar pieces of eight, and the "old rix dollars of the empire," the same value; and various other enumerated coins at a value stated, according to their weight and fine-

* Dog dollars were Dutch thalers, which had on them a figure intended to represent a lion, but more resembling a dog, and hence were popularly called dog dollars.

ness. She declares, by the advice of her council, that after the
first of January next, no Seville, pillar, or Mexican pieces of eight,
though of the full weight of seventeen pennyweights and a half,
shall be passed or taken in the colonies or plantations at above the
rate of six shillings per piece, and other silver coins in the same
proportion. A few years later these same provisions were embraced in an act of Parliament, but the proclamation was referred
to as fixing the standard up to the Revolution.

Bills of credit were afterward issued by this standard, each denomination being stated to be of the value of a specified number
of ounces, pennyweights, and grains of plate, six shilling bills, the
equivalents of pieces of eight or dollars, being of the value of
seventeen pennyweights and twelve grains of plate ; the word plate
being apparently used as equivalent to coin.

When, and how pieces of eight, came to be commonly called
dollars, does not distinctly appear. The name was derived from
Germany, there called thaler, in Denmark daler, and early translated in England, into dollar. The German *reicht thaler* was of
the same value originally as the Spanish piece of eight reals, a
real being the unit of the Spanish money of account. The Spanish
and Mexican pieces of eight, the coin most in use, were probably
soon spoken of as dollars. The first mention of them that has
been discovered, occurs in the sixth volume of the *Records of the
Province of Rhode Island*, where, in 1758, the pay of some troops
ordered to be raised, is stated in dollars, and this designation is
repeated in subsequent years. In 1763 a petition was presented
to the legislature of Pennsylvania, from which it appears that a
person living in Maryland had given his bond to a Philadelphia
trader, for the payment of a sum of money in "Spanish dollars."
There is no reason to doubt that this designation was in common
use at an earlier date than these records indicate, and it is certain
that in Philadelphia and elsewhere, a "Spanish milled dollar" was
the standard of value until after the new coinage by the Federal
government.

Several of the colonies established mints for themselves. In
Massachusetts, shillings, sixpence, and threepence, were coined as
early as 1652, by a reduction of weight, made to be of two pence
in the shilling less value than the English coin, but expected to pass
for the same. Maryland issued some silver coins in 1662, and copper half pennies were coined in Carolina, Virginia, and New Jersey,

besides a few penny and two penny pieces. The British Crown stopped all this coinage except that of copper.

The laws of Great Britain and the provincial acts punishing counterfeiters of coin, applied only to gold and silver coins, so that copper coins were frequently made by private individuals. One Mark Newbie was an early immigrant who settled in Gloucester County, and was a member of the Assembly and councillor in West Jersey. A law in that province, passed in 1682, provided that Mark Newbie's half pence, called Patrick's half pence, should pass for a half pence, current pay of this province. A large number of them had been coined in Ireland, and he continued the coinage in New Jersey. A report to the New York Assembly in 1787, states that various kinds of copper coins were in circulation of very different intrinsic values, viz: a few genuine British half pence, a number of Irish half pence, a very great number of very inferior and lighter half pence, called Birmingham coppers, made there, and imported in casks, and, lately introduced, a very considerable number of coppers of the kind that are made in New Jersey, many of them below the proper weight of the Jersey coppers.

American traders, especially in the Middle States, were as much dissatisfied with Queen Anne's proclamation, as the English merchants were with the colonial rates. Gov. Cornbury suspended its operation in New York, and the other colonies practically disregarded it. In fact it appeared then, as it is well known now, that no proclamation or statute can prevent the sale of coin for what it is worth for the purposes of trade, be that more or less than the legal rates. In 1708 the legislature of New York passed a law fixing the value of silver coins at eight shillings per ounce troy; but, notwithstanding the law and proclamation, the dollar weighing seventeen and a quarter pennyweights passed for eight shillings, and with some immaterial fluctuations this remained the current rate.

Such, indeed, was the scarcity of coin that there was a great call in the colonies for the issue of paper money, the doing of which was resisted by the British Board of Trade, to which all questions relating to the currency were commonly referred by the crown. It was only on special emergencies, that the governors, who were restrained by stringent instructions, would sanction them. The first act passed in New Jersey was in 1709, and authorized the issue of bills to the amount of three thousand pounds, for his majesty's service, some of which remained in circulation six or eight years, but were sunk by being paid in for taxes. In 1716 an act passed for the currency of bills of credit to the amount of eleven thousand six hundred and seventy-five ounces of plate, or about four thousand pounds proclamation money, which were soon paid in and redeemed.

After much controversy between the Assembly and Governor Burnet, the former refusing to provide for the support of the government, unless bills of credit were allowed, an agreement was come to in 1723, by which, as the governor wrote to Lord Carteret, the Assembly "provided for ten years to come for supporting the government, in order to obtain paper money, which their necessities made inevitable." This act authorized the issuing of forty thousand pounds in bills of various denominations, from three pounds down to a shilling. The preamble makes a long recital of the hardships of his majesty's good subjects within this colony, and states that though they had enough of the bills of credit of the neighboring provinces, yet to pay the small taxes for the support of the government, they have been obliged to cut down and pay in their plate (including, as is believed, silver coin), ear-rings and other jewels. Four thousand pounds of these bills were directed to be paid to the Treasurers of East and West Jersey, for the redemption of old bills of credit and other purposes. The rest were put into the hands of loan commissioners in each county, who lent the money on mortgage of real estate, and on deposits of plate, at an interest of five per cent. per annum, for periods not exceeding twelve years. The bills were made a legal tender, and heavy penalties were denounced against those refusing them on a sale of lands or goods; and a stay of execution was provided for, until the bills had been six weeks in the hands of the commissioners. All the bills were to be redeemed and cancelled within twelve years.

Subsequent laws provided for other issues, amounting in all, previous to the Revolution, to about six hundred thousand pounds. The last act, which was passed in 1774, was not assented to by Governor Franklin until an interval of ten years had withdrawn most of the previous issues from circulation, and not without great difficulty. The bills under this last act bore date March 26th, 1776, and constituted the principal part of the circulation of the State at the commencement of the war. Had the loan system, which had been adopted about the same time in Pennsylvania with

signal success, been rigidly adhered to, the bills would probably
have never depreciated, and would have been easily redeemed.
But some of the acts authorized bills for the expense of the war
with France and other exigencies, and these were only redeemable
by taxes which often bore hard on the resources of the colony.
Many of the laws proposed by the Assembly were refused the
assent of the governor, without which no act could pass, and some
that were assented to by him, the crown refused to sanction.   It is
said by Gordon, in his History of New Jersey, that at one time
these bills were at a discount of sixteen per cent. in exchange for
the bills of New York, and contracts in East Jersey were therefore
commonly based on New York currency.   Ebelin, a German his-
torian, whose work has not been translated, states, in reference to
New Jersey, " Paper money was first issued in 1709 ; it had a double
value; that which circulated in East Jersey had the New York
value, and in the western part of the State it was the same as in
Pennsylvania.   In the former, the guinea was valued at one pound
fifteen shillings; in the latter, one pound fourteen shillings.   This
paper money circulated in New York as well as in Pennsylvania,
therefore debts could be paid with it in either province."   According to this statement, New Jersey bills passed for a higher rate in
York than in Philadelphia.   And this is corroborated by the correspondence of Gov. Morris, who also several times mentions the
difficulty he had in negotiating bills of exchange on London, for
want of a sufficient quantity of currency in specie or in bills to
supply the ordinary necessities of Pennsylvania and New Jersey.
He says, bills for one hundred pounds sterling sold for sixty per
cent. in 1741, which was the most he could get in Jersey money.
It may be, however, that at one time the New Jersey bills were at
a discount in both cities.   In 1760 an act was passed authorizing
the Treasurers (for until after the Revolution there were always
two) to receive the taxes in money as it should pass in the western
division of the colony ; and in 1769 an act was passed reciting
that 347,500 pounds in bills had been struck for the use of the
crown in the last war against France, and that the sum of one hundred and ninety thousand pounds remained due, therefore directing
this amount to be levied in proportionate taxes yearly till 1783,
the payment to be made in money as it now passes in the western
division of the colony.   As the bills were all proclamation money
and receivable for taxes in all parts of the State, this provision

must have been applicable to payments in coin, requiring them to be received at the rate of seven shillings sixpence to the dollar, and not at the rate of eight shillings.

The bills of 1709 were in the form following, viz : " This indented bill of —— shillings, due from the colony of New Jersey to the possessor thereof, shall be in value equal to money, and shall be accordingly accepted by the Treasurer of this colony, for the time being, in all public payments, and for any fund at any time in the Treasury. Dated New Jersey the 1st of July, 1709. By order of the Lieutenant-Governor, Council and General Assembly of the said Colony." They were signed by four persons named in the law, or any three of them.

The bills authorized by the act of 1723 differed from those before issued. They commenced, " This indented bill of   ounces of plate due, &c." Three pounds were declared equal to eight ounces fifteen pennyweights of plate, and one shilling equal to two penny-weights twenty-two grains of plate, and others in the same proportion. Afterwards the form was, " This bill by law shall pass current in New Jersey for   ounce   pennyweights and grains of plate."

The bills issued by virtue of the act of 1774 were of the following form: " This bill of one shilling proclamation, is emitted by a law of the colony of New Jersey passed in the fourteenth year of the reign of his Majesty King George the third. Dated March 26, 1776," and were signed by any two of seven persons named.

The bills of 1780 were as follows, viz: " The possessor of this Bill shall be paid —— Spanish milled dollars by the 31st day of December, 1786, with interest of like money, at the rate of five per centum per annum, &c.," and had an indorsement that the United States insured the payment.

The bills issued pursuant to the act of 1781 were of the following form : " State of New Jersey. This bill shall pass current for   agreeably to an act of the legislature of this State passed January 9, 1781."

All the varieties were printed on coarse paper, with common type and various devices including, previous to 1780, the arms of Great Britain, and were easily counterfeited, which the penalty of death was found ineffectual to prevent.

The market price of silver in Philadelphia, which until within the last century was a more important emporium of trade and had more capital than New York, and, therefore, gave its law in this matter to the greater part of this State, is stated to have been per ounce from 1700 to 1739 various rates from 6s. 10d. to 8s. 9d. The full weight of a dollar, according to Queen Anne's proclamation, was 17½ pennyweights; but the provincial usage, finally sanctioned by law, was to reckon it at 17¼ pennyweights. If 17¼ pennyweights were worth 7s. and 6d., an ounce was worth something over 8s. 8d. Most of the dollars in circulation did not weigh more than 17 pennyweights.

Paper money was issued in Massachusetts as early as 1690; in New York and New Jersey 1709; and in Pennsylvania in 1723; but the subject was a constant source of controversy with the government in Great Britain. The lieutenant-governor of New York wrote to the Duke of New Castle in 1740, that the proclamation and act of Parliament were not enforced; paper bills are the only money circulating in New York. In 1746 Alexander and Morris wrote to the duke, that the officers of the government of New Jersey had been without any support or salaries to enable them to execute their offices ever since September, 1744, which they conceived was chiefly occasioned by the council and late governor's refusal to pass an act for making forty thousand pounds in bills of credit, which was at several times, passed by the Assembly, and often refused by the council or governor, because they conceived it would tend greatly to the destruction of the properties of the people of New Jersey and of all his Majesty's subjects, and because at that time the frauds and abuses of paper money in the plantations were under the consideration of the British Parliament.

In 1743, Gov. Lewis Morris, of New Jersey, wrote to Gov. Shirley, "Our paper bills being to be destroyed at stated times every year, and the interest to be paid in that specie every year, makes it necessary for the borrowers to have them, and if they have them not, to give an extraordinary price for them. The mercantile folks in York and Pennsylvania, and those that keep money in Jersey, have found their account in this. One effect has been that those in Y. and P. choose to be paid for what they sell rather in Jersey currency than their own; a second that the Jersey people rather choose their own currency than that of their neighbors; and as N. Y. and Pennsylvania cannot well manage their trade without the help of Jersey, so they must have in many cases Jersey currency to its nominal value, with respect to New York, it being now between 12 or 13 per cent. better than that, and likely to rise higher. But with respect to gold and silver its real value is much short of its nominal value, and probably always will be so while it is in the power of merchants to put what value they think proper upon gold and silver. In a Pennsylvania Gazette of Sept. 1742, the merchants of Philadelphia, to the amount of seventy-five, published at what rates they will take gold and silver, and after mentioning at what prices they will take gold (which not being fixed by act of Parliament they may perhaps have the liberty of doing), they set the value of French crowns and Spanish milled pieces of 8, at 7s. 6d. and all good coined Spanish silver at 8s. 6d. the ounce. Tho' I believe by the merchants' private agreement amongst themselves, they have always done the same thing since the existence of a paper currency, yet I do not remember so public an instance of defying an act of Parliament."

The amount of bills issued in Pennsylvania was never excessive. The greatest amount in actual circulation was about 1759, when it was stated to be 185,000 pounds. The early notes and indeed all that were issued up to the Revolution, maintained their credit very well, and but for the expense of the war they would have been redeemed at par. In 1753 a struggle began between the Assembly and the Governor which lasted many years. In 1775, Governor Morris, son of Lewis Morris, states in an angry message to the Assembly of Pennsylvania, "I said the act of the 6th of Queen Anne for ascertaining the rates of foreign coins in America was shamefully slighted and disregarded in this province, and I say so still. It is known to you and every one that Spanish pieces of eight, do now and for a number years have passed and been current at 7s. 6d., when that act requires that they should pass for six shillings only; and that other coins are current nearly in the same proportion; from whence it appears that though you call your paper bills, money according to Queen Anne's proclamation, it is really not so, but twenty-five per cent. worse."

In 1764 the Board of Trade in London made a report to the Crown, in which they assigned six reasons for restraining the emissions of paper bills of credit in America, as a legal tender, one of which was that an act of Parliament restraining and regulating the practice in New England had a good effect. Dr. Franklin, who was then the agent in London for Pennsylvania and New Jersey, published a paper, entitled remarks and facts relative to the American paper money, in which, with his usual ability, he attempted to answer those reasons, it must be confessed, however, with but indifferent success. He refers to the difficulties that had been occasioned by the want of a sufficient amount of coin, and the growth that had resulted from the use of paper money. In answer to the sixth reason, which was that in the middle colonies, where the paper money had been best supported, the bills had never kept to their nominal value in circulation, he remarks: " The fact in the middle colonies is really this, on the emission of the first paper money, a difference soon arose between that and silver ; the latter having a property, the former had not, a property always in demand in the colonies, to wit, its being fit for a remittance. This property having soon found its value, by the merchants bidding on one another for it, and a dollar thereby coming to be rated at eight shillings in paper money of New York, and seven shillings six pence in paper of Pennsylvania, it has continued uniformly at those rates in both provinces, now near forty years, without any variation upon new omissions ; though in Pennsylvania, it has at times increased from 15,000 pounds the first sum, to 600,000 pounds or near it. Whenever bills of exchange have been dearer, the purchaser has been constantly obliged to give more in silver as well as in paper for them." It is apparent from these remarks that silver fluctuated less in value, during the times specified, and commanded a less price in paper than is common now ; a fact which may be attributed perhaps in part to the much less activity of trade and to the greater expense and risk of sending it abroad. It is manifest, too, from this history of the currency, that the rates of eight shillings in New York, and seven shillings sixpence in New Jersey and Pennsylvania for a dollar, instead of four shillings sixpence, its real value, or six shillings its proclamation value, originated before paper was issued and in part from other causes.

The first notice of money that appears in the minutes of the general Congress of the colonies, which sat in Philadelphia, occurs June 14, 1775, when six companies of riflemen were ordered to be raised, and the monthly pay of the officers and privates is stated in dollars and thirds of a dollar. At subsequent times various amounts of money are specified in dollars and ninetieth parts of a dollar. This shows that a dollar was then understood to be equivalent to 7s. 6d. or 90 pennies. Cents or hundredths of a dollar had not yet been introduced. At this time the appropriations, paper bills and accounts of money in all the States were in pounds, shillings, and pence, and they so continued until the Federal Government established a mint. The provincial Congress of Massachusetts Bay, in May of this year, had ordered 100,000 pounds to be borrowed, and requested Congress to recommend to the several colonies to give a currency to their securities, which were bills for sums not less than four pounds, promising to repay on the first of June, 1777, the money "in Spanish milled dollars at six shillings each." What influences induced the Congress at Philadelphia to keep their accounts and make their appropriations in dollars and ninetieths does not appear, and can only be conjectured.

On the 23d of June, 1775, the Congress resolved to issue paper bills, from one dollar to twenty dollars each, to the amount of two million of dollars. They entitled the bearer to receive—Spanish milled dollars, or the value thereof in gold or silver. July 29th they fixed the quotas of tax each colony was directed to provide to sink its proportion of the bills. Bills of a less denomination than a dollar were first directed to be issued Feb. 21, 1776, and were for one-sixth, one-third, one-half and two thirds of a dollar. Various measures were from time to time adopted to keep up the credit of the continental currency. In June, 1776, Congress requested the several legislatures of the colonies to pass laws punishing counterfeiters. January 14, 1777, they recommended the legislatures of the States to pass laws to make the bills issued by Congress legal tenders; that debts payable in sterling money be discharged with continental dollars at the rate of 4s. 6d. per dollar, and all other debts at the rate fixed by the respective States for the value of Spanish milled dollars. The legislature of New Jersey, as early as September 20, 1776, had made the continental bills a legal tender, and made it a felony punishable with death to counterfeit them or the bills of the United States of North America. This law said nothing about the rate at which they were to pass, so that they became legally a tender at the rate of a dollar for six shillings. But an assembly which sat at Haddonfield, Feb. 11, 1777, provided that in all payments and dealings, Spanish milled dollars weighing 17 pennyweights, 6 grains, should pass at the rate of seven shillings and sixpence lawful money of this State a dollar, and that continental paper bills should be deemed in value equal to the same, except in debts due and payable in British or sterling money, in which case they should pass at the rate of four shilling and sixpence. The legislature of Pennsylvania passed a similar law, January 29, 1777. Up to this time, the rate at which the bills of both provinces were legally to pass was six shillings the dollar ; but coin was always worth more. When bills nominally for dollars came to be made a legal tender as well as those in pounds and shillings, it became absolutely essential to designate the relative value they should bear. Neither kind would purchase coin at its nominal rate, and very soon the continental money declined in value, even relatively to the provincial money.

The New Jersey act of 1777 declared that the Portugal gold half Johannes, weighing nine pennyweights, should pass for three pounds or eight dollars. This half joe, as it was familiarly called, which began to be coined about 1727, must have by this time become the most common gold coin in circulation. The provincial attorney-general, Cortland Skinner, was in the habit of selling a nolle prosequi in assault and battery cases for one of them, and lawyers reckoned their fees in the same coin, until long after the Revolution.

In December, 1777, Congress, by way of aiding the circulation of the continental bills, after reciting that it was the uniform practice of our enemies to pursue every measure which may tend to distract, divide, and delude the inhabitants of these States, to effect which they have promoted associations for supporting the credit of the public money, struck under the authority and sanction of the King of Great Britain, and thus sap the confidence of the public in the continental bills, they Resolved, that it be earnestly recommended to the legislative authorities of the respective States forthwith to enact laws, requiring all persons possessed of any bills struck on or before the 19th of April, 1775, to exchange them for continental bills or bills of the respective States. This recommendation was not complied with in New Jersey until June 8, 1779, when an act was passed declaring that the colonial bills should continue to be legal tenders until the first day of September then next, and no longer except for taxes, and that all such bills not brought into the treasury before the first day of January then next, should be forever after irredeemable. In consequence of this act some of the bills issued under the act of 1774, became valueless in the hands of the holders, and were never redeemed.

At the commencement of the war Congress had no money, and no resource but a resort to paper bills. For a year these were nearly equal to gold and silver, but the quantity they were obliged to emit exceeded what had been the usual quantity of the circulating medium. They began therefore to depreciate, as coin would, had it been thrown into circulation in equal quantities. But not having, like gold and silver, a value in the markets of the world, the depreciation was more rapid and far greater than could have happened with them. Legal tender acts, and all other extraordinary measures for the support of excessive issues of paper money, were found to be worse than useless. In two years the continental paper money had fallen to two dollars for one, in three years to four for one, and in the six months following, that is to say, in 1779, it had fallen to twenty for one. At this time a circular letter was addressed by Congress to their constituents, signed by their President, John Jay. It dwelt on the future resources of the country, and insisted upon their ability to make good all their engagements, and even went so far as to urge "that paper money is the only kind of money which cannot make itself wings and fly away. It remains with us, it will not forsake us, it is always ready and at hand for the purpose of commerce or taxes, and every industrious man can find it. On the contrary, should Great Britain, like Nineveh, and for the same reason, yet find money, and escape the storm ready to burst upon her, she will find her national debt in a very different situation. Her territory diminished, her people wasted, her commerce ruined, her monopolies gone, she must provide for the discharge of her immense debt, by taxes to be paid in specie, in gold or silver, perhaps now buried in the mines of Mexico or Peru, or still concealed in the brooks or rivulets of Africa or Hindostan."

But neither eloquence nor patriotism could hinder the operation of those laws of trade, which, like the law of gravitation, are the laws imposed by the wise Creator of the universe, and remain unchanged and unchangeable. The depreciation continued, so that in March, 1780, Congress, admitting that their bills had increased in quantity beyond the sum necessary for a circulating medium, and wanted specific funds, to rest on for their redemption, and were then passed by common consent, at least 39-40ths below their nominal value, recommended the States to bring them in by taxes or otherwise, at the rate of 40 dollars for one Spanish milled dollar, and that the States issue bills redeemable in six years, with five per cent. interest, their payment to be guaranteed by the United States.

This recommendation was followed partially by most of the States; by Pennsylvania in June, 1780. The legislature of New Jersey, by act of June 8, 1780, authorized the issuing of 125,000 pounds of bills in dollars, and in January, 1781, an act was passed reciting that great inconvenience and embarrassment may arise in consequence of none of the bills of 1780 being of less denomination than one dollar, and therefore directing that the sum of thirty thousand pounds of equal value should be issued in bills of credit, viz., twenty thousand each of ten different denominations, from seven and sixpence to sixpence each. Both these emissions were known afterwards as the issue of 1780, and remained for a long time of greater or less value, being receivable in taxes at par, and after a time at a discount.

The total amount of continental bills issued amounted in September, 1779, to two hundred millions of dollars. During the year 1780 they depreciated so rapidly, that at the beginning of the year 1781 they ceased to circulate and died in the hands of their possessors. The total loss to the community, although for the time great, was not so large as might be supposed. Allowing for the depreciated value of the bills when they were issued, it was estimated that the actual loss to the people did not much exceed thirty-six millions of dollars; and this loss fell, not suddenly, but by gradual depreciation through several years, so that it did not much, if at all exceed, what, had Congress possessed the power of taxation, would probably have been directly raised in that way. Mr. Jefferson calculated the actual expense of the eight years of war, from the battle of Lexington to the cessation of hostilities, to have been about one hundred and forty millions, or about seventeen and a half millions of dollars for each year. The contrast of this expenditure, with that incurred in suppressing the late rebellion (not less than a thousand million each year) is very suggestive.

An act of this State passed January 5th, 1781, declared that the continental currency should be a legal tender only at its current rates; and in June, a scale of depreciation was established for the adjustment of debts previously contracted, which was somewhat altered in December. By another act, passed in June of this year, it was recited that the several compulsory acts heretofore passed to support the credit of the paper money have not answered the good purposes thereby intended, and the acts making the bills a legal tender were repealed. This act provided that in case of any suit before May 1st, 1782, the debtor might tender in open court the bills of the State at their nominal value, which should be a good discharge of the debt provided that the creditor might demand security for his debt, and if the debtor neglected to give such security, he should be deprived of the benefit of the tender. It appears that the Continental as well as the State bills were very extensively counterfeited. The freeholders of this county, in 1781, allowed the several collectors eleven hundred and forty dollars for counterfeit money received.

In December, 1783, after the peace, the legislature, at the request of Congress, passed an act to raise a revenue of thirty-one thousand two hundred and fifty-nine pounds, five shillings, equal to one million five hundred thousand dollars, yearly, for twenty-five years, to be applied in payment of the interest and principal of debts due by the United States. One of the sections of this act, after reciting that it will be impracticable to raise the whole or any considerable part of said sum in gold or silver, enacts that bills be printed to the amount of the aforesaid sum, of denominations from two shillings and sixpence each, to six pounds, to be received as equivalent to gold and silver in payment of said taxes. The collectors and treasurers were directed to exchange gold and silver they might receive for said bills, and all bills paid into the treasury were to be cancelled. In 1786 these bills were made a legal tender, and were called lawful paper money.

In December, 1784, the sum of ten thousand pounds was required by law to be raised by tax, to be applied towards the sinking of bills of credit, to be paid in gold or silver, or bills of 1780 and 1781, at the rate of three dollars of bills for one of specie. In 1786 bills to the amount of one hundred thousand pounds were issued, to be loaned out, interest to be paid annually for seven years, and then one-fifth to be redeemed yearly. In 1787, it was enacted that no money should be received by the commissioners of the loan offices, or the treasurer, except gold and silver, and bills under the acts of 1783 and 1786. In 1788 it was directed that money paid into the loan offices should not be re-loaned.

Loan offices were first established in this State, in 1723, commissioners being appointed for each county, at first by the legislature, afterwards by the boards of justices and freeholders, in some

10

counties two, and in others three, who were constituted corporate bodies. A specific amount of the bills was apportioned to each office, a certain sum being retained to replace those torn and defaced. The money was loaned at one time for twelve and at others for sixteen years, at five per cent. interest, on mortgage security, the interest and a portion of the principal to be returned on the 25th of March, yearly. The whole principal might be re-paid on this day and re-loaned; but the annual payments of the principal were sent to the treasurer's office to be cancelled, or as was afterwards directed, cancelled by the Board of Freeholders. In 1735 wheat was authorized to be received at the rate of four pence less in value than market price in New York, for the eastern division, and at Philadelphia for the western division, to be re-sold for bills. Gold and silver were to be received at the rates prescribed in Queen Anne's proclamation. The bills were not only made legal tenders, but heavy penalties were provided for refusing them in payment of debts or produce. Penalties were also enacted for asking or taking any advance or discount on these bills, for bills of New York and Pennsylvania. The business of the loan office in this county was not finally closed until the year 1801.

The act of 1783 was repealed in 1790, and the tax law of this year requires the taxes to be paid in gold and silver, or notes of the Bank of North America. In 1796 such of the bills as were receivable for taxes, were directed to be paid by the treasurer in gold and silver.

It appears by the proceedings of the Board of Freeholders of this county, in 1792, that a settlement had been made with John Mulford, who had been the county collector, and that the sum of 144 pounds, 13s. 4d. had been found due to him in old State money. Ebenezer Elmer having been appointed by the board to procure this money, reported that he had obtained the same at the following rates, viz: 9s. 3d. old State money, at two for one, 92 pounds 12s. 6d., at 16s. 6d. for 20s. and 51 pounds, 11s. 7d. of lawful money at 8s. the dollar; the cost of £144 13s. 4d. being 125 pounds 2d. It would seem that all the State bills were redeemed except some of the old emission of 1776, and a small part of the bills of 1780. As early as 1779 an act had been passed declaring that the old bills should not be a legal tender after September of that year, and if not brought into the treasury by the first of January next, then they should be irredeemable. The old State money referred to in the settlement with Mulford, comprised the bills of 1780, and the lawful money the bills of 1786.

The first bank established in the State was the Newark Banking and Insurance Company, incorporated in February, 1804, and authorized to have a branch in Jersey City. In December, 1804, The Trenton Banking Company was chartered. In 1807, the New Brunswick Bank, and afterwards banks were authorized, in other places. The notes of these institutions, together with those issued by the banks of Philadelphia, New York, and other cities, formed a large part of the circulating medium of the State. They maintained the specie standard until the war with Great Britain from 1811 to 1815, when they depreciated at one time to a discount of thirty cents on the dollar, but during all this time gold and silver remained the true standard of value, and no attempt was made to make the paper of the general government, or any other paper, a legal tender.

This very imperfect review of the state of the currency during our colonial state and afterwards, will aid us in appreciating the advantages we have derived from the currency established by our present general government, in freeing us from the complicated rates, and inconvenient moneys of account, prevailing in different sections, whatever may be the result of the recent renewal of a paper legal tender currency, as compared with gold and silver, or paper convertible into coin. Mr. Adams, in his report on the subject of weights and measures, made in 1820, remarks: "It is now nearly thirty years since our new moneys of account, our coins and our mint, have been established. The dollar, under its new stamp, has preserved its name and circulation. The cent has become tolerably familiarized to the tongue, wherever it has been made, by circulation, familiar to the hand. But ask a tradesman or shopkeeper in any of our cities what is a dime, or a mill, and the chances are four in five that he will not understand your question. But go to New York and offer in payment the Spanish coin, the unit of the Spanish piece of eight, and the shop or market man will take it for a shilling. Carry it to Boston or Richmond, and you shall be told that it is not a shilling but a ninepence. Bring it to Philadelphia, Baltimore, or the city of Washington, and you shall find it recognized for an eleven penny bit, and if you ask how that can be, you shall learn that the dollar being of ninety pence, the eighth part of it is nearer to eleven than any other number; and pursuing still further the arithmetic of popular denominations, you will find that half of eleven is five, or at least, that half of the eleven penny bit is the fipenny bit, which fipenny bit at Richmond, shrinks to four pence half penny, and at New York swells to six pence."

One of the articles of the Confederation, which lasted from 1778 to 1789, authorized Congress to regulate the alloy and value of coin struck by their own authority, or by that of the respective States. The Constitution vested the right of coinage solely in the general government. Early in 1782 a report on the subject of coinage was made to Congress, by Robert Morris, said to have been the work of his assistant, Governeur Morris. He proposed as the unit the fourteen thousand four hundred and fortieth part of a dollar, which was found to be a common division for the different currencies in use; ten units to be one penny, two pence one bill, ten bills one dollar (about two thirds of a Spanish dollar), ten dollars one crown.

No steps were taken to carry this proposition into effect. In 1784 Mr. Jefferson reported the plan afterwards adopted. He took the dollar as the unit, to be of silver, a tenth or dime of silver, and a hundredth of copper. In 1785 Congress unanimously resolved, that the money unit of the United States of America be one dollar; that the smallest coin be of copper, of which 200 shall pass for one dollar, and that the several pieces shall increase in decimal ratio. In 1786 they resolved that the money of account should be mills, of which 1000 shall be equal to the Federal dollar; cents, of which 100 shall be equal to the dollar; dimes, 10 of which shall be equal to the dollar; and dollars. Eventually, as is well known, this mode of keeping accounts was adopted throughout the Union, except that mills and dimes were dropped, and the accounts were simplified by being expressed only in dollars and hundredths. The final arrangements for establishing a mint and issuing coin were not adopted until 1792. The coins authorized were of gold, eagles of ten dollars, half and quarter eagles; of silver, dollars, half dollars, quarter dollars, dimes or ten cents, half dimes; of copper, cents and half cents. At later dates one, three, twenty, and fifty dollar pieces have been coined in gold; also two cents in copper, the half cent having been discontinued.

The adoption of the dollar was recommended by the circumstances that it was a very convenient value, was a familiar well known coin in all parts of the Union, with which the money of account in use was everywhere compared, and would therefore be well understood and readily adopted. The easy mode of reckoning by decimals was convenient, and capable of being soon understood by all classes. The origin of the mark $, for dollars, is still a subject of dispute. .Some have supposed it to be an imitation of the pillars, circled by a wreath, others a combination of U S; and others, with more plausibility, the figure 8 crossed like the £, used for pounds. There seems no reason to doubt, however, that it was adopted in imitation of the same mark used in Portugal, and in some of the West India Islands. Its origin there we have no means of determining. It was not used in the United States until after the adoption of the Federal coinage. The Rhode Island minutes of the date 1758 are printed with this mark, but an examination of the original manuscript proved that it was not then employed, but the word dollars, or the contraction Drs. The earliest manuscript containing it, that has been discovered, was made in 1795, and the earliest printed book in 1801. After this it became universal; but how it was first introduced, and whether any special means were used to recommend it, seems unknown.

Accounts were generally kept in this State in pounds, shillings, and pence, of the 7s. 6d. standard, until after 1799, in which year a law was passed requiring all accounts to be kept in dollars or units, dimes or tenths, cents or hundredths, and mills or thousandths. For several years, however, aged persons inquiring the price of an article in West Jersey or Philadelphia, required to be told the value in shillings and pence, they not being able to keep in mind the newly-created cents or their relative value. Even now, in New York, and in East Jersey, where the eighth of a dollar, so long the common coin in use, corresponded with the shilling of account, it is common to state the price of articles, not above two or three dollars, in shillings, as, for instance, ten shillings rather than a dollar and a quarter. So lately as 1820 some traders and tavern keepers in East Jersey kept their accounts in York currency.

Towards the close of the Revolutionary War a considerable number of French crowns, worth $1.10, and smaller French silver coins, were introduced by the French army, and continued to circu-

10*

late for several years; and since, the French five-franc piece has circulated to some extent. The principal coins, however, in common use, continued to be the Spanish and Mexican dollars, and halves and quarters, especially the latter; Spanish and Mexican pistareens, which generally passed for twenty cents, although worth only about seventeen cents; the Spanish or Mexican real or bit, called an eleven penny bit or shilling; and its half called a five penny bit or sixpence. Prices of small articles were adjusted to these $12\frac{1}{2}$ and $6\frac{1}{4}$ cent coins in use, and so continued until within a few years. About ten years ago these current coins had become so much worn as to be worth not much more than ten cents and five cents, and for a short time passed at those rates; but the American dimes and half dimes having been coined to a considerable amount, they came into common use, and prices were slowly adjusted accordingly.

During the present century the principal circulating medium has been bank notes and silver. The gold coin from the American mint having been made of a little more relative value than the silver, was used for exportation, so that very little was in circulation until after 1837, in which year the gold coins were reduced in comparative value, and a few years ago were quite plentiful. The banks were obliged to suspend the redemption of their bills during the war commenced in 1812, and for near ten years there was very little coin in use, small change being supplied at first by the bills of individuals, and then by those issued by banks and incorporated cities.

In 1815 a temporary law of this State was passed, which provided that unless the plaintiff in an execution would consent to receive current bills of a bank there should be a stay of the proceedings. It remained in force about eighteen months; would probably have been held contrary to the Constitution of the United States, but the question was not raised. The banks have suspended several times since for short periods of time. Shortly after the breaking out of the Rebellion the government of the United States issued large and small bills, and enacted laws declaring them to be a legal tender in payment of all debts.

The legal interest of money in this State was eight per cent., until 1738, when it was reduced to seven per cent. per annum. In 1774 an act was passed lowering the rate to six per cent., but it was disallowed by the crown. The change to six per cent., which now prevails in most of the State, was made in 1833. Some of the eastern cities and counties have special laws authorizing seven per cent.; and appearances indicate that the latter rate will have to be adopted in all parts of the State.

In 1866 an act passed raising the interest to seven per cent throughout the State.

INDEX

This new index cites all people mentioned in the text, as well as the place names and topics from the original index.

_____, Alexander 49 Clarence 51 Daniel 19 Edmund 17 Ephraim 26 38 John 49 Nicholas 17 Owen 47 Richard 56 Smith 51 Thomas 78 William 19 49
ACTON, Benj 17
ADAMS, Elizabeth 21 John Q 57 Mr 135
ALEXANDER, 126
ALISON, Dr 99
ANDREWS, 96 97 102 Jedediah 96
ARMSTRONG, Edward 18
AYLMER, 98 John 98
AYRES, Caleb 94 Jona 31
Antioch, 20
Area and acres of county, 89
Assembly members of, 32
BACON, 13 Jeremiah 102 Samuel 13
BAPTIST, 90-95 Seventh day 94
BARKSTEAD, Joshua 17 47
BARROW, Zachariah 12
BASSE, Jeremiah 47
BATEMAN, Ephraim 32
BELL, John 77
Beller's survey, 18
BELLERS, 19 Helby 18 John 18
BENNETT, Jeremiah 34
BENSON, 110
BERESFORD, John 70
BERKLEY, 7
BILLINGS, Edward 7
BLAIR, 103
BLOOMFIELD, Dr 61 67 Gov 61 68 Joseph 15 56 67 Mr 69 Mrs 61
BODLEY, 77 Mrs 77 110
BOON, Enoch 27 41 42
BOUDINOT, Elias 15

BOWEN, 32 David 16 34 90 Elijah 64 94 Jonathan 32 41 51 93 94 Mr 94 Sheriff 15 Smith 27 54 William S 28 66 Wm S 28
BOYD, 42 Martha 52 Mr 26 45 Mrs 45 52
BRADSTREET, Mr 96
BRAINERD, David 105 John 105
BRICK, John 18 32 77 Joshua 32 77
BRIDGE, Cohansey 16
Bridges of county, 23 83 of Indian field tract 47
BRIDGES, 48 96 John 47 Thomas 47 95
Bridgeton city of, 28 38 105
BRINTON, Mr 75
BROOK, 90
BROOKS, 91 Henry 73 Jonathan 115 Mr 94 Rev Mr 93 Timothy 90 William 115
BROWNE, Joseph 12
BUCK, 26 32 Dr 54 Ephraim 39 66 Jeremiah 25 35 50 John 34 Joseph 34 81 Mr 56 81 Mrs 26 46 43 Robert S 34
BUCKINGHAM, Daniel 104
BUDD, Eli 79 110 John 17 72 Thomas 18 29 Wesley 79 110
BURCH, James 41 42 52 53
BURGIN, Enoch 34 George 28 34 39 40 Reuben 34 42
PURNET, Gov 123
BUTCHER, William 91
BUTLER, John 12 23
BYERLY, Thomas 18 72
CADWALLADER, Gen 75
CAMPBELL, David 34

www.ingramcontent.com/pod-product-compliance
Lightning Source LLC
Chambersburg PA
CBHW071802090426
42737CB00012B/1915